The Post-Civil War Spanish Social Poets

Twayne's World Authors Series

Janet Pérez, Editor of Spanish Literature

Texas Tech University

TWAS 686

The Post-Civil War Spanish Social Poets

By Santiago Daydí-Tolson

University of Virginia

Twayne Publishers • *Boston*

The Post-Civil War Spanish Social Poets

Santiago Daydí-Tolson

Copyright © 1983 by G. K. Hall & Company
All Rights Reserved
Published by Twayne Publishers
A Division of G. K. Hall & Company
70 Lincoln Street
Boston, Massachusetts 02111

Book Production by Marne B. Sultz
Book Design by Barbara Anderson

Printed on permanent/durable acid-free
paper and bound in The United States
of America.

Library of Congress Cataloging in Publication Data

Daydí-Tolson, Santiago.
    The post-civil war Spanish poets.

    (Twayne's world authors series; TWAS 686)
    Bibliography: p. 160
    Includes index.
    1. Spanish poetry—20th century—History and
criticism.   2. Literature and society—Spain.
I. Title.   II. Series.
PQ6085.D37 1983   861'.64'09   82-21178
ISBN 0-8057-6533-6

Contents

About the Author

Santiago Daydí-Tolson teaches Latin American literature at the University of Virginia. He holds a professional degree from the Universidad Católica de Valparaíso (Chile), and the Ph.D. from the University of Kansas. He has received awards from the Woodrow Wilson Fellowship Foundation, The American Philosophical Society, and the University of Virginia. His publications include articles on Spanish social poetry and on Latin American authors, including Mariano Azuela, Gabriela Mistral and Ernesto Cardenal. Mr. Daydí-Tolson has contributed to the *Columbia Dictionary of Modern European Literature,* and is the editor of *Vicente Aleixandre: A Critical Appraisal,* a scholarly volume devoted to the work of the latest Spanish Nobel in literature; he is also the editor of *Five Poets of Aztlan,* a collection of contemporary Mexican-American poets.

Preface

Spanish literary life during the Republic and the Civil War years was manifestly ruled by politics. While the conservative writers upheld the traditional values of a Catholic and imperial Spain, the Republican writers claimed democratic freedoms, social justice, and the basic human rights. The military triumph of the conservatives did not put an end to the dispute; it only suppressed it temporarily. The early postwar years witnessed the overt use of poetry as propaganda for the new regime's basic ideologies. In a markedly politicized world, poets accepted as the norm the instrumental and utilitarian value of literature in the development of a national conscience and public attitudes.

What we now call Social Poetry was a consequence of the political conception of literature, and of Spain's immediate historical circumstance, a revived expression of the continuing fight between conservative and left-wing ideologies, which had only apparently been ended by military force and political power. Social Poetry represents a view politically and aesthetically opposed to that of the writers who supported Franco's autocratic rule, a form of protest within the bounds which censorship imposed.

A complete survey of social poetry in postwar Spain would have to include a much larger number of pages and references than the ones offered in this introductory study. In view of selectiveness and representativeness, only a few poets have been taken into consideration. Particular attention has been given to Blas de Otero and Gabriel Celaya, undoubtedly the most prominent and characteristically "social" poets in the period. For the other cultivators of social lyrics, I have preferred a more limited treatment. A few have been studied individually; others have been included in a group, particularly when it has seemed better to analyze their similarities and correspondences rather than their differences. This has been the case especially with the younger poets, whose works show signs of a common view on reality and exhibit certain similar aesthetic preferences.

THE POST-CIVIL WAR SPANISH SOCIAL POETS

Since the objective of this book is to offer a critical literary interpretation of social poetry in postwar Spain, the most effective approach would be analytical rather than purely descriptive. All citations from the original poems have been translated with the purpose of providing the reader with a strictly literal version as an aid in reading the Spanish texts. Prose quotations are provided only in English. Notes and bibliographical entries are limited to the most basic titles.

Santiago Daydí-Tolson

University of Virginia

Chronology

1939   End of the Civil War, with the triumph of the Nationalist forces. Antonio Machado dies on 22 February in Colliure, France.

1940   First issues of the literary review *Escorial*.

1942   Miguel Hernández dies in prison.

1943   First issue of the poetic review *Garcilaso*.

1944   Dámaso Alonso, *Hijos de la ira;* Vicente Aleixandre, *Sombra del paraíso;* first issues of the poetic review *Espadaña*.

1946   The United Nations recommends the diplomatic isolation of Franco's regime. The book of poems *Pueblo cautivo* is published underground in Madrid. First issues of *Insula*.

1947   José Hierro, *Tierra sin nosotros* and *Alegría*. Gabriel Celaya, *Tranquilamente hablando*.

1949   The Holy Office decrees excommunication to Communists and leftists. Gabriel Celaya, *Las cosas como son*.

1950   End of Spain's isolation. The United Nations authorizes the resumption of diplomatic relations with Franco's regime. Blas de Otero, *Angel fieramente humano*.

1951   Harsh governmental censorship under the direction of Gabriel Arias Salgado, new Secretary of Information and Tourism. First manifestations of popular unrest: general strike in Barcelona. Blas de Otero, *Redoble de conciencia;* Gabriel Celaya, *Las cartas boca arriba*.

1952   *Antología consultada de la joven poesía española;* Miguel Hernández, *Obras escogidas,* including his poems written in prison; José Hierro, *Quinta del 42;* Gabriel Celaya, *Lo demás es silencio*.

1953   Spain signs pact with United States and concordat with the Vatican; full recognition of Franco's regime.

1954   Vicente Aleixandre, *Historia del corazón*.

1955   Spain becomes a member of the United Nations. Vicente
        Aleixandre, *Algunos caracteres de la poesía española contem-*
        poránea; Blas de Otero, *Pido la paz y la palabra;* Gabriel
        Celaya, *Cantos iberos;* José Agustín Goytisolo, *El retorno;* José
        Angel Valente, *A modo de esperanza.*

1956   Student riots at the University of Madrid. Gabriel Celaya,
        De claro en claro; Angel González, *Aspero mundo.*

1957   Gabriel Celaya, *Las resistencias del diamante;* José Hierro,
        Cuanto sé de mí and *Poesía del momento.*

1958   Blas de Otero, *Ancia;* J. A. Goytisolo, *Salmos al viento.*

1959   Intellectuals and writers pay homage to Antonio Machado
        in Colliure, France. Gabriel Celaya, *Cantata en Aleixandre;*
        Blas de Otero, *Parler Clair* (published in France).

1960   Gabriel Celaya, *Poesía y verdad* (essays) and *Poesía urgente* (in
        Buenos Aires); José María Castellet, *Veinte años de poesía es-*
        pañola; José Angel Valente, *Poemas a Lázaro.*

1961   Gabriel Celaya, *Los poemas de Juan de Leceta,* first volume of
        the Colliure poetry series. Angel González, *Sin esperanza, con*
        convencimiento; J. A. Goytisolo, *Claridad.*

1962   Slight change in censorship under new direction of Manuel
        Fraga Iribarne. Vicente Aleixandre, *En un vasto dominio;*
        Gabriel Celaya, *Espisodios nacionales;* José Hierro, *Poesías com-*
        pletas (1942–1962); Angel González, *Grado elemental* (pub-
        lished in Paris).

1963   Blas de Otero, *Esto no es un libro* (published in Puerto Rico);
        José Angel Valente, *Sobre el lugar del canto; Poesía última,*
        edited by Francisco Ribes.

1964   Blas de Otero, *Que trata de España* (published in Paris).

1965   Alfonso Sastre, *Anatomía del realismo;* Leopoldo de Luis, *Poesía*
        social. Antología (1936–1965).

1966   José Angel Valente, *La memoria y los signos.*

1967   Victoriano Crémer, *Poesía total;* Angel González, *Tratado de*
        urbanismo; José Angel Valente, *Siete representaciones.*

1968   José Angel Valente, *Breve son.*

1969   Blas de Otero, *Expresión y reunión* (1941–1969); Gabriel
        Celaya, *Poesías completas;* José Manuel Caballero Bonald, *Vivir*
        para contarlo (complete poems).

1970 Juan Carlos de Borbón officially declared Franco's successor. Blas de Otero, *Mientras;* Gloria Fuertes, *Antología poética* (1950–1969); José Angel Valente, *Presentación y memorial para un monumento* and *El inocente* (published in Mexico).

1972 Angel González, *Palabra sobre palabra* (complete poems); José Angel Valente, *Punto cero* (complete poems).

1973 Gabriel Celaya, *Dirección prohibiba* (published in Buenos Aires); J. A. Goytisolo, *Bajo tolerancia.*

1974 Blas de Otero, *Verso y prosa* (anthology); José Hierro, *Cuanto sé de mí* (complete poems).

1975 Franco dies on 20 November. Jaime Gil de Biedma, *Las personas del verbo* (complete poems).

Chapter One

First Manifestations of Social Poetry in Postwar Spain

The first manifestations of a socially inspired poetry in postwar Spain must be related to the movement toward the *rehumanization* of poetry that began to emerge around the mid-1940s. This renewed interest in concrete human experiences and feelings was less the result of a politically committed conception of poetry and the poet than the emotional response to the difficult experiences suffered during and immediately following the Civil War. It is important insofar as it presupposes an aesthetic view of a more humane sort opposed to the formalism practiced by many postwar poets.

The Immediate Postwar Period

When in the spring of 1939 the Civil War ended with the triumph of the Nationalist armies, repressive effects were strongly felt in the intellectual and literary life of the country. The decade preceding the war had been characterized by social and political turmoil, and by the increasing public involvement of writers and poets in ideological confrontation. The war itself originated a fully committed literature on both sides of the conflict;[1] at the end of the war, one side was totally silenced—at least inside Spain—while the other side was free to engage in the full development of its views—political and aesthetic. These were, for poetry, initially, the formulaic imitation of an artificial neoclassical style remindful of the imperial past revived under the triumphant flags of nationalism. This pseudoclassical revival *(Garcilasismo),* inspired in the grandiose ideas of an Imperial Catholic Spain—bastion of Western civilization in a world of moral, social, and political decadence—followed very nearly the ideological basis upon which Franco's dictatorship sustained itself: exaltation of God and Motherland.

Two representative periodicals—*Escorial* and *Garcilaso*[2]—exemplify the early postwar subsidized poetry that tried rather uninspiredly to reproduce the classical sonnets, tercets, and other metric forms which poets of the Generation of 1936 had already turned out in admiring imitation of the Golden Age masters.[3] Little of what these neoclassical poets wrote during the immediate postwar period is of interest today; it had limited interest even among Spaniards of the period, since a reaction was soon to come in the form of a more sincere expression of deeply felt personal conflicts, directly related to historical circumstances. From this individualistic first manifestation of an interest in the real surrounding world to a more socially and politically minded literary commitment was but a step; and once this step was taken, the formalism of the neoclassical poets was quickly forgotten.

The year 1944 has been commonly accepted as the starting point for a new poetic awareness with its corresponding stylistic and thematic singularity. During that year were published Vicente Aleixandre's *Sombra del paraíso* [The Shadow of Paradise] and Dámaso Alonso's *Hijos de la ira* [Children of Wrath], as well as the first issues of a new poetic journal, *Espadaña*. Not all of these publications should be considered genuinely social in inspiration, in spite of later critical support of the idea that these were the generators of the new literary orientation.[4] Neither Aleixandre nor Alonso actively supported a socially committed conception of poetry; as for the editors of *Espadaña*, they did not necessarily agree on a theory of literary commitment, although they were inclined to favor a poetry critical of the political and social circumstances.

A Paradise Lost

Leopoldo de Luis's interpretation of Aleixandre's *Sombra del paraíso* as representative of the postwar Spanish exile stresses the historical value of its images and the emotional state of those who considered themselves defeated: "The attitude of the poet is that of disenchantment. . . . Earth has opened up and has swallowed a loved vital reality. A terrible war has just finished, and the poet writes this book as a cosmic consciousness of the devastation."[5] The image of the lost paradise is then the adequate one to express the feeling of bereavement experienced by Spaniards who had lived in a better world and had seen it disappear.

Still, in his analysis of the book the critic could have also stressed the literary topic of infancy, a common and characteristic theme among social poets. *Sombra del paraíso* gives a nostalgic view of a past time when the boy lived in a landscape of natural greatness and beauty. There is in these poems a sense of loss—underlined by the use of contrasting tenses and adverbs of time and space—that prefigures the emotional attitude characteristic of several poets much younger than Aleixandre.

"Primavera en la tierra" [Spring on Earth][6] develops the topic in strikingly effective images. The years of youth are represented by an almost pagan view of the world inhabited by "Spirits of a higher heaven," and by the personified Spring. Insisted upon is the image of light "illuminating my brow in the fertile days of youthful happiness." The world itself "resounded in the yellow glory/of the changing light." In this paradisiacal world the speaker remembers himself as a naked boy, the utmost expression of human purity.

At the end of the poem, the past tense changes to the present, transforming the entire circumstance:

Hoy que la nieve también existe bajo vuestra presencia,
miro los cielos de plomo pesaroso
y diviso los hierros de las torres que elevaron los hombres
como espectros de todos los deseos efímeros.

Y miro las vagas telas que los hombres ofrecen,
máscaras que no lloran sobre las ciudades cansadas,
mientras siento lejana la música de los sueños
en que escapan las flautas de la Primavera apagándose.

(Today that snow also exists under your presence. I look at the skies of sorrowful lead and see the irons of the towers built by men as if they were the ghosts of all ephemeral desires. And I look at the imprecise fabrics offered by men, masks that do not cry over the tired towns while I feel far away the music of my dreams in which the flutes of Spring run away as if they were flickering out.)

The present is characterized not only by the loss of youth, but also by the disappearance of all that was natural and beautiful in Paradise, particularly light and nakedness. There is no direct indication that the present world corresponds to the actual circumstances of postwar Spain, as there is no proof that the paradise of youth is pre-Franco

Spain. The poet develops in this poem an idea he has been working upon since before the war.[7]

Infancy, for Aleixandre, represents that paradisiacal period of life at the origins of mankind. Maturity and the actual world signify the fall of man, and the consequence is expulsion from paradise. This vision of infancy as a primal, happy state, and the consequent disillusionment of growing up, have points of contact with one of the frequently reiterated motives of social poetry: the memories of infancy, and the sudden fall, or awakening, to the world, caused by the war and its terrifying experiences. The experience of the war did not "awaken" Aleixandre, who had been born much earlier than those social poets whose infancy and youth coincided with the years of the conflict. The actual biographic truths of the memories of the poet's boyhood in Málaga indicate no intentional criticism of recent Spanish history in *Sombra del paraíso.* At most the book expresses, in deeply symbolic terms, the state of nostalgia for a better place and time now definitely lost.

Aleixandre's direct influence in the development of social poetry in postwar Spain comes a few years after the publication of *Sombra del paraíso,* and as a result of his theoretical understanding of poetry as a form of human communication. After the war Aleixandre was seen by younger poets as a master, the representative of a generation dispersed by the war, the generation of García Lorca and Alberti, Guillén, and Salinas. All of them, and many more poets and intellectuals, had either died or left the country because of their political and social beliefs. Aleixandre stayed, and his "neo-romantic" poetry appeared as the alternative to the classically formulaic poetry advocated by the politically conservative groups.[8]

Sombra del paraíso represents in Aleixandre's work an evolution toward more concretely human subjects. His previous books were characterized by strongly emotive images that rarely touched the immediate experience of man; the poet dealt with deep levels of subconsciousness, and his subject matter was too abstract and hermetic to be understood without difficulty. With the poems of *Sombra del paraíso,* the surrealistic imagery is changed in favor of more direct, more immediately experienced images and situations. The marked emotional overtones of the voice are another aspect of Aleixandre's work that helped to create a sensibility for more urgent realistic subjects.

A Child of Wrath

Another member of the Generation of 1927, Dámaso Alonso, also had a certain influence on the growing trend toward social poetry. His *Hijos de la ira* achieved an impact in the Spanish literary world primarily because it appeared at a moment when the public was fully prepared to receive a book of its characteristics. It was not only an original treatment of a particular subject, but the expression of a human experience much like that of all Spaniards at the time. No one could have failed to see his own personal circumstance reflected in the highly subjective poems of Alonso. His tormented voice was that of each reader, the voice of hundreds of individuals faced with a world of despair, pain, and anguish.

This community of feelings and experiences, and the contemporary historical basis for the poet's cry, are the reasons for later interpretations of the book as an initial step into social poetry. Alonso himself pointed to the fact that his book was the first to voice a protest; but, although he likes the idea of being at the beginning of a poetic movement, he is careful enough to explain his wider interests, thus avoiding any misinterpretation of his true objectives as a poet: "I have said several times that *Hijos de la ira* is a book of protest written in Spain at a time when nobody protested. It is a book of protest and questioning. Against what does it protest? Against everything. It is useless to try to consider it as a particular protest against specific contemporary facts. It is a much wider protest: a universal, cosmic protest that includes, of course, all those other partial wraths."[9]

It is quite obvious that in Alonso's poetry there is no intention of formulating any specific social protest. "I wrote *Hijos de la ira,*" he declares, "while filled with disgust at the 'sterile injustice of the world' and totally disillusioned with being human." The seemingly political reference to injustice in the world is too vague to indicate a true commitment to bettering the social problems of the world, or even those of Spain. His disillusionment with the world is based on the idea of the fall of human nature, and revolves around the conception of God's justice. The conflict is presented mainly in personal and existential terms, with the few obvious generalizations for the collectivity of men. Man, the individual, is nobody but the author himself.

Alonso's lack of profound social awareness is attested by vaguely uncommitted references to the contemporary world in general and by his preoccupation with himself, expressed in the intentional use of the author's own name in several compositions. When Alonso names himself, he does so in anger, disdain, or self-mockery, because he accuses himself of human weaknesses and sinfulness. In doing this, the poet stresses the main point of the book: the conviction concerning man's sinful nature—which explains the situation of the world—and the individual's despair because of his own fallen nature. It is, in short, a self-centered book, an egotistical prayer with the dramatic recourse of Christian self-debasement before God, in a desperate move to obtain mercy.

Alonso's poetry belongs most properly to a type of literature quite different from the social mode. The introduction of a clear reference to immediate historical circumstances in *Hijos de la ira* does not suffice to make it a historically conscious book, as some would like to believe. The line "Madrid is a city of more than one million corpses (according to the latest statistics)" (*P.E.*, 79), cannot be interpreted as referring to the Civil War and its many dead. The corpses are the actual inhabitants of Madrid in that year, 1944, who are figuratively dead. The poetic statement has little or nothing to do with the social or political circumstances in Spain at that moment or before. Death represents in this poem the spiritual state of modern man, including the poet, who has been dead for a lifetime: "At times in the night I turn over and sit up in this niche where for forty years I have been rotting away."

The immediate turn to God in the same poem sets the tone for the rest of the collection:

> Y paso largas horas preguntándole a Dios, preguntándole
>   por qué se pudre lentamente mi alma,
> por qué se pudren más de un millón de cadáveres en
>   esta ciudad de Madrid,
> por qué mil millones de cadáveres se pudren lentamente
>   en el mundo.

(And I spend long hours asking God, asking him why my soul is slowly rotting; why more than a million corpses are rotting in this city of Madrid; why billions of corpses rot slowly in the world.) (*P.E.*, 79)

Aleixandre's vision of a fallen man finds its counterpoint in this cemetery-world. Both poets are good friends, and Alonso, an enthusiastic reader and critic of Aleixandre's works, must have read, by then, *Mundo a solas* [Lone World], a book written by Aleixandre before *Sombra del paraíso* but published only in 1950. This book offers as a central image a world in which man has died. But Aleixandre does not take God, or any other particular transcendent view of man, into consideration. For him it will be fruitful to discover the essential truth of everyday subjects totally immersed in concrete reality. Alonso, instead, follows a religious tradition of spiritual transcendence and gives a dramatic account of man's fight against annihilation and despair.

At a time when religious or seemingly religious poetry was the norm in Spain, a book like *Hijos de la ira* could not pass unnoticed. It dealt with a basically identical subject of other poems of the day, yet the approach was different. First, the attitude of the speaker was emotionally more complex and true to life than that of other religious poets. Accordingly, the poetic expression differed greatly from the stiff, regulated patterns preferred by the other poets. Alonso's compositions do not follow any previously established form; the voice expresses with no restraint the most striking emotions, in a rhythmic and lexical freedom bordering on everyday language. Images and vocabulary are taken from the ugliest aspects of reality, thus contrasting briskly with the selected images and vocabulary of the epoch's pseudoclassical poetry, which was filled with angelical and rhetorically empty beauty. [10]

In essence, the differences are the consequences of different attitudes toward reality. The rage, despair, and emotional tone of Alonso's poems could be seen as characteristic of the social poets' diction. Consequently, it is easy to suppose Alonso's influence on the development of style. If the social poets make use of certain poetic techniques similar to the ones used by Alonso, it is because of their personal emotional protest against unjust society. The coincidence is largely formal, and thus the influence of Alonso's work should be termed tangential.

Hijos de la ira is a major work of a talented poet and, as such, offered new solutions, new possibilities of expression for Spanish poetry of the period. Whatever effect it had on the future of Spanish poetry was because its poetic language and attitude provided an alternative to the formalism of subject and style practiced by con-

formist poets. Alonso introduced new emotions, making explicit
a tone of voice and an attitude that everyone could equate with deep
individual feelings. His book was the perfect one for that particular
period—it acted as a catharsis and opened the way for experimen-
tation with other forms of expressing an interest in the common
man and his difficult circumstances.

Espadaña

More directly responsible for the development of social poetry in
Spain was the literary journal *Espadaña,* published in León from
1944 to 1951. Its editors did not have a clear editorial line and
published a rather indiscriminate miscellany of poems and criticism
of various types. Among these were the first texts of socially inspired
poetry, and some critical comments directed toward a theoretical
formulation. Of no less importance is the fact that it was also in
its pages where the Spanish reader could find texts by Vallejo,
Neruda, and Hernández and criticism concerning Spanish poets in
exile.[11]

With a printing of only 250 copies per issue, *Espadaña* did not
have a large readership; and it is easy to imagine that those interested
were mostly the poets and writers who collaborated in the same
magazine, together with a few other readers of poetry. In one of the
first issues Antonio G. de Lama—the priest and critic responsible
for the creation of *Espadaña*—comments upon the public for whom
the journal should be intended. Recognizing that poetry is essentially unpopular, the privilege of a select minority, he hopes to
widen the circle of these select few by including the "intellectual
class . . . formed by professionals who have a more or less ample
culture, but are ignorant of poetic culture."[12] In later issues Victoriano Crémer and Eugenio de Nora—the two poets in charge of
the publication—express quite different, and more radical, ideas.

Like de Lama they realize that poetry in Spain is an art for a
privileged class. Unlike him, they see this characteristic as a negative
and unacceptable one. Poetry should be concerned with man, the
common man who knows no privileges of class; and, obviously, it
should reach him and express his views of the world, his attitudes
and emotions. Nora and Crémer want to be themselves poets of the
people: ". . . we would particularly like to see our verses picked
up by the people, picked up and sung by them; we would like to

see that our verses were part of their emotional outlook; and if we were able to express in our own verses some of what the people feel, of what they would like to express, of what profoundly moves them . . . we will consider ourselves true poets."[13]

This view of poetry as an expression of the people's concerns underlaid the main objective of *Espadaña* from the start—to help in the rehumanization of contemporary poetry. A year before the publication of the first issue of the journal, de Lama wrote an article that has been termed the first manifesto of *Espadaña;* criticizing the lack of vitality among the young Spanish poets, he called for less formalism and more human warmth in contemporary poetry: "but has not that sharpness of expression taken away all substance from poetry, transforming it in rhetorical play, in nothing but verbal juggling? It is because of it that it is desirable to find in modern poetry a little less of form and a little more of life. Less stylistic perfection and more shouts. Less metaphors and more shouts . . . Life, life, life. Because without it everything is dead (obvious axiom)."[14]

The article was published in *Cisneros,* a student publication at the University of Madrid, of which Eugenio de Nora was editor. His agreement with de Lama's ideas is further proved by a poem published sometime later in *Espadaña.* The first two stanzas compare formalism to death, as de Lama had contraposed formalism to life:

> Existen muchas leyes como estatuas
> en tierra derribadas, abolidas,
> y otra vez luego en pie, fantasmas fríos,
> trabas, mordazas, bridas.
>
> Sobre tantos modelos, normas quieren,
> extensos cementerios habitando;
> en lo libre, la luz, no lo olvidemos,
> espera, está esperando.

(There are many laws, monuments that had collapsed and have been abolished to stand later again, cold ghosts, ties, gags, reins. On top of so many laws they want norms, while they live in large cemeteries; in freedom—let us not forget—light waits, it is waiting.)[15]

For Crémer poetry is dead because it lacks human interest: ". . . poets have abandoned the distinguished habit of risking themselves eagerly . . . poetry in our time . . . . is a poetry without faith and without hope, and it is born dead even from the same thought that originates it. And it is useless to try to do anything to revitalize it. It is quite dead—in spite of its youth—and stinks like an old corpse."[16] The lively and emotive shouting demanded by de Lama is also considered a need by Crémer: "It will be necessary to scream out our present verse against the four walls, or against the fourteen bars of the sonnet, with which young men as old as the world pretend to encircle and strangle it."[17] Identical liking for loudness is shown by de Nora in the last stanzas of his poem:

¡No lo olvidamos, nunca olvidaremos!
Así, pues, vivos, fieles a un destino,
el verso apasionado descorchamos
libérrimo y sin tino.

Entre álamos mecidos y aire verde,
escapándose fúlgido al combate,
el verso vaya fiel en el misterio,
fiel siempre al hombre, al corazón que late.

(We do not forget it, we will never forget it! Alive, then, and faithful to a destiny, let us uncork the passionate, free, and careless verse. Among swinging poplars and green air, let the verse go running aflame to the combat, faithful to the mystery, faithful always to man, to the heart that palpitates.)

While they were strongly against the kind of literary creation practiced in Spain at that moment, they were not able to effect any meaningful transformation in Spanish contemporary lyrical language. They did call attention to the need for a more human poetry that later developed naturally into a social concern, but they did not create a new poetic language. At most, they tried to emphasize emotions by mere rhetorical exclamations, and by means of a few supposedly shocking images or expressions.

Victoriano Crémer

Of the two poets responsible for the publication of *Espadaña,* Victoriano Crémer is the elder. Born in 1909 he actively participated in the Civil War and was strongly affected by its outcome. In spite of his age he had published before the war only one book, which he does not subsequently include among his works. It was only after the defeat of 1939 that he turned to literature in a more determined way, undoubtedly because of intervening political developments and their social consequences.

Crémer was not a member of the middle or upper class, as many intellectuals are in Spain, and was particularly sensitive to the problems of his own class. He even had been a member of the Anarcho-Syndicalist party. Knowing his theory of poetry as a form of biography, it is easy to understand why a man who had been actively involved in the politics of social justice turned to poetry once his freedom of action had been curtailed. "Poetry," he writes, "is always, always, always a form of biography. He who is faithful to himself will write the type of poetry that corresponds to his most unfailing vital throb, to his deepest memories, to his most fruitful demands."[18]

Because of his strong feelings about the subject of his interest, Crémer's works suffer from the excessive rhetoric of *tremendismo.*[19] Subjects, images, words, and expressions are negatively exaggerated. In an effort to dramatize the injustices of man against man, he overemphasizes the attitude of the speaker and prefers techniques akin to declamation. Even his conceptions are reduced to basic opposing forces easily represented by starkly evident images and symbolic representations. Consequently, his poems tend to be rather verbose and unstructured. Crémer's first recognized book, *Tacto sonoro* [Sounding Touch], was published in 1944; it contains two poems inspired by the war, an indication of the poet's interest in the historical circumstances. Another composition has as its subject the capture and death of John Dillinger, seemingly a popular hero. In all these poems, the political and social consciousness of Crémer is quite evident.

In "Canción para submarinos" [Song for Submarines][20] the regular stanzas of four octosyllabic verses with alternate consonant rhyme, and the short couplets between them, are all directed to create the light and fanciful composition of a child's song. The images, and a general conception of the submarine as another creature of the sea, and more so the comparison with a buccaneer, collaborate in creating a playful idea of the submarine; the last stanza, without any change in the tone or quality of the previous verses, offers an unexpected reality that points directly to a concrete contemporary fact—the submarine war in the Atlantic: "Tu colmillo, / ciego de plata lunar, / va dejando un reguerillo / de sangre sobre la mar . . ."("Your fang, blinded by the silver of the moonlight, is leaving a tiny trickle of blood on the sea . . .").

Several of Crémer's poems follow this same pattern of composition: the structure, tone, and imagery of a popular, almost childlike song, only slightly marred by a notion of pain, death, or injustice. On the other hand, a composition like "Oda malherida del avión en picado" [Badly hurt ode for the falling plane, *P.T.*, 49–51] represents another type of poem, an altogether different one in structure, tone, and poetic devices. This longer composition uses free verse, and tries to dramatize the war bombardments through a highly rhetorical and inflated style. The beginning of the poem provides an indication of what follows for fifty-nine lines:

> ¡Oh!, gran violador del aire, tú, Arcángel bravo.
> Elegido de los dioses.
> Carbonizado por la pura palabra de quien sostuvo el mundo
> cuando el sol ignoraba el fragor de su vientre.

(Oh!, great rapist of the air, you, brave Archangel. The one chosen by the gods. You have been charred by the sole word of the one who sustained the world when the sun was ignorant of the tumult in its womb.)

Besides selecting rather meaningless images the poet fails in the syntactical clarity of the text, so that the reading could lead to any number of interpretations. In a similar way, the reasons of the speaker to suppose that there is no escape from the falling plane are not quite convincing:

> Es porque sé que tú,
> —Angel exterminador, Luzbel sin esperanzas—
> te abrazarás conmigo y con mi muerte
> en el estruendo ciego . . .
>   . . . junto a un lirio manchado por mi sangre
>   y una carta de amor ahogada en gasolina.

(It is because I know that you—Exterminating Angel, hopeless Lucifer— will embrace me and burn with me and my death in the blind commotion . . . by a lily that has been marred by my blood, a love letter drowned in gasoline.)

This tendency for excessive images of death and destruction, this simplified vision of reality in two-toned opposing forces, pervades all of Crémer's work, rendering difficult an aesthetically convincing reading. "Fábula de la persecución y muerte de Dillinger" [Fable of the Persecution and Death of Dillinger, *P.T.*, 58–63] combines both kinds of poetic compositions with the added element of narration. Narrative stanzas alternate with simple songs and apostrophic discourses characteristic of Crémer's inordinate sense of drama. The topic in this poem is not at all new: the opposition between the forces of a corrupt capitalist society and the heroic figure of the individual who tries to break the system only to be used by it as a new capital value:

> Y en el Club del banquero Vanderwilde
> —sudorosas papadas en reposo—,
> subastan un sombrero verde claro
> en millares de dólares.

(And in the club of Vanderwilde, the banker—sweating fatness in repose— a light green hat is auctioned for thousands of dollars.)

The poem is structured in several sections divided in groups of different voices (voice of the wind, of the air) and journeys (or acts), a type of organization that precedes the *cantatas* of Celaya. The sections of predominantly traditional songlike stanzas, with their expressive animations and popular images, are an important factor in the poem, lending movement and popular flavor to a story otherwise heavy with exaggeration. Unfortunately, Crémer does not make good use of this aesthetic possibility, and in his following books prefers the more elevated style, not his most effective. As the actual editor of *Espadaña,* Crémer published his poems in the journal with regularity. Among them is a fable about a popular Spanish hero, "Fábula de B. D." [The Fable of B. D., *P.T.*, 78–85], a long poem that seems more verbose than Crémer's other compositions. In this fable he tries to narrate the execution of Buenaventura Durruti, the Spanish anarchist leader, without naming him directly, for obvious political reasons. The political commitment is carefully disguised in a pompous series of images appropriate to any hero, and in vague allusions to the real circumstances. Still, the poem contains several strong notes of criticism concerning the political and social climate in Franco's Spain.

The wickedness of the socially unjust system is represented by two images in Crémer's works: night and darkness are common to practically all social poets; the city, as center of social oppression, is more peculiar to him,[21] although most social writers will make reference to it. Both images are combined in "La fábula de B. D.":

> Si no fuera que el sol, despavorido,
> enciende los tejados
> y su rejón de fuego se derrama
> sobre el manso recinto amurallado,
> diríase que duerme la Ciudad
> desde siempre: que sueñan su trabajo
> los millares de seres que recorren
> infatigablemente el mismo itinerario,
> corrompidos de buenos pensamientos;
> que es noche todo el día y que ese fardo
> de sombra y de silencio y de morirse
> soñando que se vive, sin soñarlo,
> es eterno.
>
> El hombre se resigna
> y la Ciudad, se duerme, boca abajo.

(If it were not for the sun that, frightened, lights the roofs and throws its spear of fire over the calm and wall-enclosed place, one would say that the City sleeps since forever: that the thousands of people who walk indefatigably the same itinerary corrupted by their good thoughts, dream their work; that it is night all day long, and that the bale of shadows and silence and of death dreaming with life, without dreaming, is eternal. Man is resigned to it, and the City falls asleep, face to earth.)

An actual enumeration of other topics forms a section of twenty long, free verses. Crémer uses a technique preferred by the social poets because of its oratorical quality—the anaphoric repetition of a pattern with occasional slight modifications to avoid monotony. In this particular case the poet has selected as the initial repeated formula a phrase from colloquial speech, "Porque sucede que . . ." ("But it so happens that . . ."). The expression is loaded with meaning—in this case the inevitability of the human condition. There is no need to insist on the negative characteristic of all the observations: man is a condemned being, much as Alonso said in his poems; man's defects are many and include injustice and deceit, two motives well repeated among social poets: "Porque sucede que la Verdad es una vieja coima aletargada / como un oscuro sapo, al sol. Que la Justicia es una dueña zurcidora." ("But it so happens that Truth is an old bribe, slumbering, like a dark frog, under the sun: That Justice is an old mending Celestina").

Injustice is represented in the murder of good men by the powerful few who are socially and morally invaluable. These are the two classes that clash:

> Porque sucede que la tierra es un destartalado Cementerio
> donde almacena el hombre sus muertos inservibles;
> porque los muertos válidos, los elocuentes muertos,
> se hacen junto a las tapias o en las hondas cunetas
>   solitarias.

(But it so happens that earth is an unkempt cemetery where men stock their useless dead; because the only valuable dead, the eloquent ones, are those beside the walls or in the deep and lonely gutters.)

Between 1944 and 1949, Crémer published four books, of which *Caminos de mi sangre* [Roads of My Blood, 1947], *Las horas perdidas* [The Lost Hours, 1949], and *La espada y la pared* [The Sword and the Wall, 1949] were clearly inspired by a desire to discuss Spain and her political and social situation. In the last of these books, a series of poems under the title "Canto total a España" [Total Song for Spain] exemplifies the then common obsession with the motherland.

His *Nuevos cantos de vida y esperanza* [New Songs of Life and Hope, 1951], received the Boscán Prize for poetry in 1952, an indication of the effect his poetry had on the reading public at that period. "Regreso" [Return, *P.T.*, 146–47] serves as a true poetic credo and explains Crémer's aims when writing these poems portraying poor people and their sufferings.

The speaker addresses a town to which he has returned: "Ya me tienes en ti de nuevo" ("I am in you again"), back from a world of empty decorations and lifeless beauty:

> Regreso del laurel y de la escayola;
> del dulce silbo, de la estrella seca;
> de un mundo de ceniza, con espejos
> de purpurina y sueño, repitiéndose.

(I am back from the laurel and the plaster; from the sweet whistle, from the dried star, from a world of ashes with mirrors made of purpurine and dreams that repeat themselves.)

The allusion is not perfectly clear by itself, but its contrast to the "walls of mud and straw," which the speaker touches with joy, juxtaposes two opposing worlds of wealth and poverty. While wealth is characterized by coldness and lack of life, poverty is full of human warmth and fertility. Back in this impoverished world the speaker finds his true essence and a purpose for his life:

> Estas son las raíces que me llegan
> al corazón; la voz que a la garganta
> desemboca; la mano que me tiende
> la copa verdadera de la sangre.

(These are the roots that reach my heart; the voice that comes to the mouth; the hand that passes me the true cup of blood.)

The idea of quasi-religious communion with other oppressed men is further developed in another stanza:

> Aquí contemplo vida, me hago llama
> de esta hoguera de manos que levanta
> sus negras lenguas a lo alto. Siento
> que soy un hombre más entre los hombres.

(Here I see life, I become a flame of this bonfire of hands that raises up its black tongues. I feel that I am just another man among men.)

This feeling of generic belonging would have sufficed to make this poem an example of social poetry; even the selection of images— cup and hands—and of the opposing worlds—ashes and fire— reminds the reader of Neruda's "Reunión bajos las nuevas banderas." The continuation, or final section of the composition, adds the final, most important aspect in social poetry—the hope for a better world. Dawn will become among social poets the symbol of this worldly faith in the future of man:

> Y un vestido de angustia me abandona
> sencillamente, así la noche deja

> desnuda el alba y libre, aunque con frío,
> cuando lejanos sones la presienten.
> Frío tengo en el alma, pero canto,
> ahora que estoy aquí de nuevo y veo
> tanto gozo y dolor, tanta miseria
> y tan clara esperanza compartida.

(And a robe of anguish leaves me unobtrusively, as night leaves dawn naked and free, although cold, when faraway sounds announce it. I have cold in my soul, but I sing, now that I am here again and I see so much joy, so much pain, so much misery, and such bright hope for all.)

After this book Crémer published other titles, but his poetry had sprung forth as an immediate emotive response to an external situation that called for his intervention. Once the motivation became less urgent, the poet seemed to have less need for writing, and his work was limited to a less creative repetition of itself. But for some time Crémer followed his conception of the poet: "The poet, I believe, cannot elude the commitment of his being human in time" (*P.T.*, 17). For Crémer, being a poet is determined by a need to express something, and by the consequent duty to say it; it is a matter of ethics rather than aesthetics: "Poetry is everywhere, invades everything, categorizes everything, with the condition that the poet will not forget his human condition, and translate, then, from his humanness, the ample and generous teaching he receives from life" (*P.T.*, 18). An altruistically impressive belief, Crémer's credo defines, more than a poetic theory, a feeling, a moral standing that is necessary before any true social poem can be born. In a similar position is Eugenio de Nora.

Eugenio de Nora

Much younger than Crémer, Eugenio de Nora, who was born in 1923, was part of the first group of university students in postwar Spain. While in Madrid he became involved in literary activities, and as editor of *Cisneros* was responsible for the publication of de Lama's article in favor of a rehumanization of lyric poetry. From the beginning he had been opposed to any form of poetry that did not pay attention to human values.[22] His activities as a poet, like those of Crémer, were closely linked to *Espadaña,* and somewhat limited to the period of preponderance of social poetry. Most of his poems were published between 1945 and 1954. His living in Switzerland, where he is a professor at the University in Bern, perhaps limited his possibilities of participation in the literary life of his country.

De Nora's poems are not numerous, and not especially satisfying as literature. More than an accomplished poet, he was the voice of an aim, of a project for a new poetry. His contemporaries must have valued this intention, since he was considered for a time to be among the best of the young poets of the period. But his writings about poetry are significantly lacking in theoretical content, and their main lines of thought are reducible to a simple formula, similar to Crémer's own: poetry is a form of personal expression of the deeply human interests of the writer; being a true spiritual need, the poet cannot escape writing it. The essentially emotive power of poetry can only be damaged by a conscious care for form; therefore, the poet has to write in simple terms, be direct, and, above all, be sincere with himself. As for the subjects, any one that presents itself to the poet as necessary to be communicated is appropriate. One thing should be asked of the contemporary poet—to sing with happiness and hope.

None of these ideas leads necessarily to the writing of social poetry. The requisite for prevailingly simple expression is, though, one of the characteristics of any text that strives for social validity; in fact, it becomes very important for the poets who want to create a style appropriate to their social convictions. De Nora himself made an effort in this direction. His social commitment is expressed in several of his collaborations with *Espadaña*. Particularly significant among them is a letter to Crémer criticizing the latter's less-than-consistent editorial policy.[23]

Espadaña had not been able to maintain its original sociopolitical objective. Any poet, including those who maintained a pseudo-classical attitude of happy conformism, or even proregime writers who proclaimed the greatness of Franco Spain, could publish in the journal. As Víctor G. de la Concha has underlined, in de Nora's attack against this lax policy there was a "will to take the rehumanization of poetry forward in the direction of social class commitment."[24]

If you want to write a poetry, a literature that [will] be humane, effective and popular, you will have to reject and to despise . . . aesthetic as well as other conventions. Above all you will have to widen greatly the thematics and the language of the poetry now in fashion, a mandarinesque world of ivory. You will have to remember that the probable readers, the public or the people, are divided in classes of ideas, taste, interests, and conceptions on life different and opposed, and that it is necessary to decide in favor of one or the other.[25]

"Un deber de alegría" [A Duty of Happiness],[26] one of de Nora's last poems in *Espadaña,* offers a good example of what he contributed to Spanish social poetry. In essence, it reproduces the same concepts and same images of Crémer's "Return." The style is unimpressive. Images are few and topical; the free verse awkwardly follows the lengthy sentences structured oratorically in appositions and repetitions; the structure of the composition seems diffuse, a problem of many poets affected by their obsession to be above all communicative.

The poem vaguely alludes to a previous time, when man suffered from existential anguish: "¿Yo fui triste?" ("Was I sad?"). Immediately comes the awareness of the world, manifested in concrete, almost sensual terms: "En la noche / siento que avanza el mundo como el amor de un cuerpo . . ." ("At night / I hear the world move on like the desire of a body . . ."). The basic image of night representing the historic present in Spain is followed by the hope of a new day to come:

> Todavía, mientras dura la noche,
> mientras la soledad, tan tuya,
> y la inmensa tristeza sedienta y sin sosiego
> de los que multiplican tu soledad en mundo
> funden—Eugenio, España—una tiniebla sola,
> todavía
> algo queda en el alma, y si aprietas los ojos
> por despertar, por no creer la sombra,
> aún fragmentos de aurora la sangre nos daría.

(Still, while night lasts, while solitude, your own, and the huge sadness, thirsty and restless, of those who multiply your loneliness in that of a world, melt—Eugenio, Spain—a single darkness, still something is left in your soul, and if you close your eyes tightly trying to awaken, to forget the shadow, still our blood would give us fragments of dawn.)

In the following stanza the subject is poor people, the workers who in their sad situation still find the smile of human care and love. The force of love among men is the strength of humanity: "Nunca sueña quien ama, nunca / está solo. La pujanza es idéntica." ("Those who love never dream, they are never alone. The inspiring force is identical"). And de Nora, like Crémer and all social poets who followed their example, awakens to reality before those people, realizing his duty as a poet: "entonces, duramente, / algo en mí se incorpora, y siento, sin remedio / un deber de alegría," ("then, something stands up harshly in me and I feel, unavoidably, a commitment of happiness"). The last image of the poem is, of course, dawn: "Y enemigo, expulsado de la tristeza, siento / cómo la aurora iza su bandera rociada" ("And enemy, expelled from sadness, I feel how dawn raises its dewy flag").

The poet has experienced a moving spiritiual transformation, something approaching religious conversion, from individual sadness to historical hope, from egotistical loneliness to communal belonging. As a natural consequence of this experience he develops an ethical sense of social duty. The intellectual and emotional process follows very nearly the same lines that characterize Neruda's change of attitude during the Civil War. It certainly corresponds to a frame of mind characteristic of the period, which would explain why the same motif is treated almost identically by different poets, and also why these poets became well known and appreciated by the Spanish reading public.

Signs of the Times

Besides the names of de Nora and Crémer, *Espadaña* included works by several other poets who during the next decade would be considered among the most representative of social poetry; among them, Blas de Otero, Gabriel Celaya, and Angela Figuera Aymerich. None of them published a socially committed text until the 1950s. During the period of *Espadaña*—that is, the six years from 1944 to 1951—Spanish writers and intellectuals began to develop a sense of awareness and responsibility toward their immediate reality, Spain. The many poems devoted in these years to the greatness or miseries of the motherland speak of the growing interest in Spain, its values, its history, its people, and the future destiny of them all. It is important to record that one of these books, *Pueblo cautivo* [Captive People, 1946], was published underground and anonymously.[27] Although its distribution must have been more limited than other books of poems, it matters here because of its historical value as a document of the period. Its being an underground publication points to the existence of governmental censorship, a fact every writer had to take into consideration; it also indicates the existence of a spirit of criticism and accusation of the injustices among at least some Spaniards. Social poetry grew from these seeds of political opposition to the government and is closely related to leftist interpretations of society and art.

Pueblo cautivo contains at least two basic topics of social poetry: the poet's moral obligation to turn away from pure poetry: "Yo bien quisiera / hablar con voz más pura de la luna y las flores" ("I certainly would like to talk with a purer voice about the moon and the flowers"); but another more important subject is waiting to be sung: "pero ahí está lo otro, / un oleaje, una salva de aplausos y disparos, / el mar ronco en las calles" ("but there it is, the other aspect, a wave, a round of applause and shooting, the hoarse sea in the streets"). The same images reappear in countless poems because they are straightforward and expressive. The second topic is related to the first one. The poet declares himself a witness of the world: "Yo soy aquel que mira" ("I am the one who observes"), and consequently, bears witness to reality: "Digo cosas que veo" ("I say what I see"). Reality, in his case, also means truth: "Todo el que pueda, oiga, porque cada palabra / que escribo está madura de verdad." ("Everyone who can listen, do it, because each word I write is filled with truth").

The social poet is already defined by these characteristics. To express them, to insist upon talking about them, becomes an obsession with him, and certainly should be considered another defining aspect of the social poet's emotional outlook on the world. The psychological state of mind that would finally produce a series of works inspired by contemporary Spain and its shortcomings as a modern society was already in formation and needed only the opportunity to expand and express itself.

Chapter Two
Effects of the War

There is no doubt that the Spanish Civil War was an experience that profoundly affected most, if not all, Spanish poets publishing in the 1940s; but only a few made negative comments about it in their works. Most of the literature related to the war, or to postwar Spain, was a conditioned response to established government propaganda to keep order in political matters by stressing patriotic greatness under God. Critical views were not welcomed, and those who harbored them either kept silent or expressed them in disguised, indirect or symbolic terms.

The Two Spains

In his sonnet "Patria" [Fatherland], Eugenio de Nora speaks to the teenagers at the start of the war. Although the poem, written in 1946, does not favor one or the other faction, the ideological conflict is implied in the second stanza:

> Pero la tierra es honda. La tierra necesita
> un bautismo de muertos que la hayan adorado
> o maldecido, que hayan en ella descansado
> como sólo ellos pueden, haciéndola bendita.

(But earth is deep. Earth needs a baptism of dead men who have loved or cursed her, who have rested in her as only they can do, making her sacred.)[1]

Love and hate, two attitudes that reappear in many social poems, could represent both sides ambivalently. The poet adds another cherished idea—that the men who died fighting, no matter for which side, did not die in vain; on the contrary, they made their fatherland a more sacred place. The reasons for this veneration of the war-torn land are beyond comprehension, and de Nora does not give any hint to understanding them. The concept seems to respond to a certain fixed formula for the reconciliation of all Spaniards.

The subject of the war's casualties at that particular moment in Spanish history must have been an obsession with those who, belonging to the losing side, had survived—their own survival being a matter of serious consideration. Ildefonso-Manuel Gil was born in 1912; therefore, he experienced the war in a more direct way than de Nora and his generation and wrote, as early as 1939, poems that dealt with defeat. His *Poemas del dolor antiguo* [Poems of the Old Pain], published in 1945, is the first book of protest to appear in postwar Spain.

The poem "La soledad poblada" [The Inhabited Solitude][2] reproduces the tone of a voice mildly emotional in its exteriorization of sad thoughts that flow in almost silent meditation. The poet has selected a structure of irregular stanzas of unrhymed hendecasyllabic verses, with abundant cases of run-on lines, to obtain the appropriate effect. The first stanza of fifteen verses opens with the image of night: "Todas las sombras de la noche nacen / en mis ojos abiertos al silencio." ("All the shadows of night grow in my eyes that I keep open to silence"). After commenting in metaphorical terms on the sadness and hopelessness of the defeated, the poem continues in more direct language:

> Tantos seres que amaba se me han ido,
> que ya mi juventud es sólo un eco
> de emociones de ayer, vueltos los ojos
> hacia un camino largo, interminable,
> cercado de altas, doloridas tapias.

(So many loved ones have left me that my youth is only an echo of yesterday's emotions; I turn my eyes toward a long, unending road enclosed by tall and sorrowful walls.)

Loneliness and prison are two penances that the defeated survivor has to endure. But those who died have given him an aim for his desolate existence:

> En la cerrada noche del insomnio,
> todo cuanto ellos al morir callaron
> me lo dicen a mí. Yo he de decirlo,
> con sus mismas palabras a vosotros,

> para hacer imposible que el silencio
> me los vuelva a matar en la memoria.

(In the enclosed night of insomnia they tell me everything that they had to leave unsaid when they died. And I have to say it, to tell it to you with their own words, so that silence will never be able to kill them again in my memory.)

The poet has an obligation to fulfill. Although Gil does not specify any ideological content at any moment, as to what those dead people left unsaid, the poem alludes to the broken dream of a particular ideological group:

> No dejaremos que la muerte siegue
> el vuelo de su ensueño y su esparanza,
> ni que ponga el olvido en nuestros labios
> una canción que apague su recuerdo.

(We will not allow death to cut down their flights of hope and daydreaming; nor are we going to let oblivion put on our lips a song that would extinguish their memory.)

For Gil, then, there is no reconciliation in sight; the fighting continues in the will to keep alive and strong the ideals of a group of people temporarily defeated. In "La muerte que se espera" [The Expected Death], it is a prisoner condemned to death who envisions his own end and comforts himself with the idea that even death will not destroy his ideals:

> Y por eso, morir con sencillo heroísmo
> es ensanchar los límites estrechos de la vida.
> Hay algo de nosotros que quedará en la tierra:
> la rebeldía última, vencedora del tiempo.

(And because of that, to die with simple heroism is to widen the narrow limits of life. Something of ourselves will remain on earth: the last rebellion, conqueror of time.)

Another writer who suffered the consequences of the ideological feud is José Hierro. Born in 1922, he published his first book, *Tierra sin nosotros* [Land Without Us], in 1946. Although the title is in itself quite suggestive, there are no direct references in the book to the war or its repercussions in Spanish life during the first years of dictatorship. When in the poem "Ellos" [They][3] the poet mentions his dead friends who "come every night to my side," no one would insist that he is referring to activists who died because of their political convictions. Contrary to Gil's resolution to preserve the memory of his dead friends, Hierro would prefer oblivion:

> Por mucho que intentara
> ocultarme, enterrarlos,
> por mucho que quisiera
> creer que está el pasado
> para siempre dormido,
> ellos, desde sus altos
> tronos, ellos, siluetas
> contra un cielo apagado,
> ellos, amigos, hijos
> del mismo tiempo, hermanos
> en el mismo dolor,
> silenciosos, doblados
> por su pesada carga
> vendrían a mi lado.

(No matter how much I might try to hide from them, to entomb them, how much I might wish to believe that the past is forever asleep, they, from their high thrones, they, silhouettes against a darkened sky, they, friends, sons of the same time, brothers in the same pain; they, quietly, bent under their heavy weight, would come to my side.)

An alert reader would see in these verses a reference to the time of the war, a painful period that the speaker wants to forget. The poem in itself, while not supporting such a reading, does not make it improbable. This procedure is characteristic of Hierro's poetry, and it is noticeable also, in different degrees of effectiveness, among other social poets. It is a form of disguise, a purely allusive kind of expression that requires from the reader a complicity with the author in its interpretation; with the absence of this cooperation the reader can obtain a meaning devoid of social or political implications.

The four people the speaker remembers in "Ellos" are not definitely shown to have died in the war or because of political activism. Pedro "Murió un día de marzo / Allá lejos . . ." ("Died a day in

March; over there, far away . . ."); Fernando "Enterrado en la
niebla / quedó un día" ("Entombed in fog rested one day"); and
Rodrigo "Murió ahogado / frente a la playa un día / de tormenta"
("Drowned in front of the beach on a stormy day"). Nothing is said
about Milagros's death, but the fact that the poet did not know her
personally could be interpreted as the extended friendship of political
camaraderie:

> Milagros:
> yo no la conocí.
> Tenía viente años.
> Dicen que eran sus ojos
> transparentes y vagos;
> que era alegre y muy linda . . .

(Milagros: I did not know her. She was twenty years old. They say that
her eyes were translucent and vague; that she was cheerful and pretty.)

While Gil and de Nora confer some meaning upon death by
seeing in it a political or social expression of man, Hierro is faced
with the total inability to understand his dead friends; their relationship with the living has been severed:

> Yo no sé qué palabras
> traen, que no he descifrado.
> Nombres, fechas, lugares . . .
> ¡Señor, me está vedado
> su secreto! No puedo
> darles mi sangre. Hablo
> con ellos y no entienden
> mis palabras. Los llamo
> a voces y no me oyen.

(I do not know the words they bring, I have not deciphered them. Names,
dates, places . . . Oh! Lord, their secret has been denied me. I cannot
give them my blood. I talk to them and they do not understand my words.
I call them and they do not hear my shouts.)

A reader unaware of the author's biographical data will not see
in this poem more than a common fact in human life—the memory
of our dead and our inability to communicate with them. But this
poem by Hierro was first published in *Espadaña,* and it is almost
certain that it was read, at least by certain people, in the context

of other poems dealing with the critical memories of the recent civil war.

De Nora's sonnet, published in *Espadaña,* and his poems "Lo que yo pienso sobre ello" [What I Think about It] and "En la muerte de un amigo" [On a Friend's Death], contain sections devoted to the effective power of death over the living. In "En la muerte de un amigo" (*P., * 161–65), the poet remembers how he and his friend used to contemplate the ruins left by the war:

> Recuerdo ahora cuánto y cómo,
> frente al azul del Guadarrama,
> entre las ruinas de la guerra
> y los brotes primaverales,
> hablamos, o miramos mudos:
> la presencia de tantas cosas
> nos hacía desvelar verdades.

(I remember how much and how we talked and looked, in silence, facing the blue of the Guadarrama and among the ruins of the war: the presence of so many things allowed us to discover the truth.)

Those who had died were also among the "so many things" that helped them open their eyes to reality and truth: "Los enterrados no emergían, / pero sí su peso, en el alma." ("The buried ones did not emerge, but their weight was felt in our souls").

A very direct criticism of the continuous killing of dissidents in Spain and the use of violence as a political weapon is the main objective of "Lo que yo pienso sobre ello" (*P., * 166–71). Within the loosely conceived structure there are a few verses in which the death of a politically committed man killed in the street acquires a meaning in history:

> Sabía que morir no es mejorar de sitio,
> pero aceptó ser puente en un camino.
>
> Así, soltando las anclas del Tiempo
> hacia el futuro, ha sido muerto.

(He knew that dying does not improve one's position, but he accepted being a bridge in a road. Thus, removing the anchor of Time toward the future, he has been killed.)

De Nora indeed was a committed writer, and more explicit in his attacks than others, but perhaps he could do it because he lived in Switzerland; neither Gil nor Hierro could risk being more direct in his protest, although in Gil's case there was a strong sense of poetic duty that makes him one of the first social poets in postwar Spain.

The Soldier

In his poem "Al soldado desconocido" [To the Unknown Soldier], Ildefonso-Manuel Gil deals with a subject related to the motif of the dead fighters, apparently influenced by a social point of view that considers the soldier as a mere pawn fighting a war in which he has little to win. Using unrhymed hendecasyllabic verses Gil manages to write a composition in which traditional literary rhythm and topics combine themselves with a contemporary view and attitude toward the subject.

The poem has almost seventy lines, most of them hendecasyllabic, grouped in twelve irregular stanzas; this irregular structure differs from the patterns preferred by most of the poets of the Generation of '36, among them Gil himself. The unrhymed verses and the irregular stanzas reduce the rhythmical stress of traditional versification and propose a reading that approaches a freer form of speech, in this case, a discursive conversation with a personified Earth:

> Porque tu impasibilidad me duele,
> quiero escuchar tu voz eterna y muda,
> oh madre Tierra, tú, que igual acoges
> la carne destrozada y el hierro que la hiere.

(Because your impassiveness hurts me, I want to hear your eternal and silent voice, oh mother Earth, you, who accept equally the torn flesh and the metal that hurts it.)

The conclusive conjunction used as the first word of the poem stresses the logical value of the speaker's attitude, while the apostrophe to a personified natural entity introduces the solemnity due a subject of so much importance. The technique is rather unoriginal, and many a poem to Spain during those years addressed in solemn apostrophic attitude the personified motherland or earth. While the apostrophic lyrical attitude has always added a dramatic tone to the speaker's discourse, it also can be overdone and fall into mere formula, emptied of any emotional value, or worse, become melodramatic, and consequently less than effective as a lyrical communication of ideas.

Gil's poem does not totally avoid the extremes. If the first stanzas are somewhat melodramatic, particularly in the selection of imagery and in the address to earth, toward the sixth stanza the speaker's tone changes and becomes truly emotional. His sincerity is made evident in the less strident images and in the conversational tone of one person talking naturally to another:

> Se llamaba . . . Nada importa su nombre.
> Había una palabra concretando
> el mundo vario y uno de su vida.
> Tenía ¿cuántos años? . . . Los que fueran.
> Tú no entiendes de nombres ni de tiempo,
> la fugaz rosa y la perenne encina
> son en ti iguales.

(His name was . . . It does not matter. There was a word that made concrete the various and only world of his life. How old was he? . . . Whatever. You do not understand anything about names or time, the shortlived rose and the eternal oak are the same for you.)

This attitude does not predominate or define the poem. In an increasingly emotive tone, produced by a series of rhetorical questions that point to the impassiveness of the earth with respect to the dead soldier, the poem reaches the final climax, introduced by a verse in which the attitude of the poet is directly described: "Airadamente te pregunto, Tierra, / ¿por qué le devoraste y lo escondiste / hecho barro en tu entraña?" ("Angrily I ask you, Earth, why did you devour him, why did you hide him inside yourself transformed in mud?").

It is this last declaration of the speaker's true feeling and the ensuing expression of his reforming idea that characterize much of social poetry, its tone and objective:

> Debía haber quedado eternamente
> como cayó, bañado en sangre y roto,
> aliento muerto y porvenir cerrado,
> sueño perdido y sangre derramada

            sobre tu impasibilidad,
                    y en vuelo
            crecer y abrirse sobre los silencios
            en hondo grito, en implacable grito
            contra la guerra, contra aquellos hombres
            duros y fríos que abren las esclusas,
            por donde corre el río desbordado
            de la sangre a los mares de la muerte.

(He should have remained where he fell forever, in your impassiveness
drenched in blood and broken, dead breath and closed future, lost dream
and spilled blood; and flying he should have grown and expanded over
the silence in the shape of a deep cry, an implacable cry against war,
against those men who coldly and harshly open the locks to let run the
overflowing rivers of blood toward the sea of death.)

The same topic is found in a poem by Miguel Labordeta, published
in *Espadaña*, "Mi antigua juvenil despedida" [My Old Youthful
Farewell].[4] This composition offers certain differences with respect
to Gil's poem, although they have a similar motive. Gil follows the
traditional forms of the Spanish verse: regular number of syllables,
rhythmically adequate accents, and, in many cases, respect for the
rhyme. An extensive use of run-on lines helps him create a sense
of uneasiness through the rhythmical breakage of the pattern; the
voice, then, does not fall into an easy sing-song or rest comfortably
in well-defined patterns. Still, the virtues of traditional metrics are
very much a part of the poem's structure and the reader can recognize
an established melody and follow it without difficulty. Images,
vocabulary, and a well-defined structure in terms of stanzas and
other metrical patterns work also as in a traditional type of composition. With Labordeta the situation is different.

More inclined to use the experimental language learned from
Vanguardism, and in particular from the Peruvian César Vallejo,
Miguel Labordeta does not write in traditional verse, and in most
of his compositions he introduces several irrational techniques, a
characteristic rather exceptional in postwar Spanish poetry. But his
poem "Mi antigua juvenil despendida," is, in a way, an exception
to his normal style—no irrational aspects come between the poem's
meaning and the reader. This clarity of expression carries a clear
message—all men are equal:

La vida es hermosa. Somos hermanos.
Nos han parido los mismos soles misteriosos.
Yo tengo mis sueños y mis dolores y mis trabajos
y mis pequeñas alegrías y mis pequeñas miserias
como tú tienes tus sueños y tus dolores y tus trabajos
y tus pequeñas alegrías y tus pequeñas miserias.

(Life is beautiful. We are brothers. We have been given birth by the same mysterious suns. I have my dreams and my pains and my hardships and my little joys and my little miseries as you have your dreams and your pains and your hardships and your little joys and your little miseries.)

Soldiers are victims of wars in which they have little at stake besides their valueless lives: "Ya es tarde para preguntar por qué y para qué / nos llevan al desolladero total" ("Now it is too late to ask why and with which purpose they take us to the total slaughter"). In addition to the motive of the soldier, this poem contains other characteristics typical of many later examples of social poetry: free verse, reiteration, clarity of expression, and the use of colloquialisms like "Déjalo. No importa." ("Just forget it. It doesn't matter") and "panaceas y mitos y queriditos ombligos" ("panaceas and myths and lovely little belly buttons"). All of these are aspects of the style that Labordeta must have learned from reading César Vallejo's later poems. They supposedly make lyrical poetry more accessible to the people, that is, the common people who normally would not read poetry, the people in whom the social poet is most vitally interested.

The seemingly oral character of the composition aims at the same objective. It is attained partly by the use of common, colloquial language and by the apostrophic attitude of the speaker, reinforced by verbs of aural perception: "Oye joven camarada terrestre" ("Listen young earthly comrade"). The recurrent structure, resembling that of a sermon or a political harangue, also indicates the poet's intention to communicate directly through oral means rather than by writing:

Oye joven camarada terrestre
joven humano desconocido
de cualquier país de cualquier raza o idioma
permite que por un momento
antes de morir en las trincheras
mientras se forman precipitadamente divisiones motorizadas

y las multitudes aún rugen en los campos de fútbol
deja que yo
veterano de treinta años de edad
escriba en tu mochila de bisoño
mi antigua juvenil despedida:

(Listen young earthly comrade, unknown young human being from any
country and any race or language, allow me that for a moment before
dying in the trenches while hastily the motorized units are formed and
the multitudes still roar at the football stadiums, let me a thirty-year-old
veteran write on your recruit's knapsack my old youthful farewell.)

In the level of its contents the poem has other topical aspects of
social poetry, like the opposition between the purity of youth and
the disenchantment of mature age, as seen in the last two verses
cited above, and also toward the end of the poem:

Pero permíteme
que por un momento en un relámpago
mientras adivino el fulgor de tus ojos aún niños
perdidos por la tierra desierta
escriba en tu mochila de bisoño.

(But allow me that for an instant while I feel the light of your still boyish
eyes lost on the desert land I write on your recruit's knapsack.)

The belief in a community of all men is obviously a motive
properly social in conception; it is related to the concept of culture
as a common possession, as it is also common to the world and all
of creation:

Son tuyos y míos los cielos y los mares y las nubes
los aires y las sangres la luz de cada día los trigos que germinan
la fe de los muertos que nos miran de lejos
su herencia en hermosas ciudades y en libros como incendios
en catedrales hasta las estrellas
maravillosas invenciones músicas azules
y en estos signos con que ensucio
tu limpia mochila de bisoño.

(They are yours and mine the skies and the seas and the clouds and the
airs and the bloods the light of every day the wheat that germinates the

faith of the dead who look at us from afar, their inheritance in beautiful cities and in books like fire in cathedrals high as the stars, wonderful inventions, blue musics, and in these signs with which I dirty your clean recruit's knapsack.)

But the beauty of all this has been marred, made meaningless by the absurd egotistical ideas and interests of a few men:

> Ya es tarde para preguntar por qué y para qué
> nos llevan al gran desolladero total
> perdieron mucho tiempo nuestros papás y tíos
> en creer doctrinas y consignas
> panaceas y mitos y queriditos ombligos.

(Now it is too late to ask why and for what purpose they take us to the great and total slaughter our fathers and uncles lost too much time believing doctrines and slogans panaceas and myths and lovely little belly buttons.)

The same poet who wrote this text, one of the less elusive of the social poems of the period, also called for a revolutionary poetry, "the poetry of men who have been born among declarations of war, [and] concentration camps."[5] But his work as a poet, published in poorly distributed editions, was not well known in postwar Spain, nor did it have much relation to social poetry in matter of content or style.

The Prison

The war left not only dead, but also survivors. These are the ones who had to face reality and consider their situation in new circumstances. Among the ones unsatisfied with the outcome of the war—mainly losers or disillusioned followers of an ideal—there is a powerful image representative of the new order—the image of the prison, strongly rooted in reality and, in some cases, in personal experience. From the highly emotive accounts of autobiographical experience in Gil's and Hierro's poems, to a symbolic conception in de Nora, the prison becomes a constant in social poetry, and understandably so.

In a dictatorship, freedom is taken from the individual in many forms, subtly and not always so dramatically as by incarceration;

but imprisonment is, without a doubt, the most distinct manifestation of man's loss of freedom, and it seems only natural that the postwar poets use it as a representation of the new political situation in their country.

In his first book, *Tierra sin nosotros* [Land Without Us, 1946], José Hierro includes the poem "Canción de cuna para dormir a un preso" [Lullaby for a Prisoner, *C.S.M.*, 44–46], which gives an idea of the poet's attitude toward the historical situation. Several are the lullabies that could be cited in comparison with this one; for instance, Hernández's "Nanas de la cebolla" [Lullabies of the Onions][6] and Crémer's "Canción para dormir a un niño pobre" [Lullaby for a Poor Boy].[7] They coincide in that they attribute to sleep a desired state of ignorance concerning the immediate circumstance.

Using a topic directly related to the loss of innocence brought by the sudden awakening of the child to an unjust world, Miguel Hernández tells his son: "Desperté de ser niño: / nunca despiertes" ("I woke up from my childhood: / you should never wake up), and closes his lullaby with a final wish: "No sepas lo que pasa / ni lo que ocurre" ("You should not know what happens / or what occurs"). For Crémer sleep helps the child to forget his hunger: "¡Uuuuuu . . . ! Duerme mi niño, / que viene el aire / y se lleva a los niños / que tienen hambre." ("Uuuuuu . . . ! Sleep, my child, because the wind is coming to take with him the boys who are hungry"). In Hierro's poem, the grown-up prisoner becomes a child. The composition interrelates two opposite situations represented by the dualities of child-man and dream-sleep. There is no absolute opposition between these factors, and consequently the final conclusion is unclear: all four aspects are confused in a vague reality akin to a dream. Of utmost importance for the understanding of this composition are a few repeated verses, with slight variation in two parts of the poem. The first time they appear contrasting the verses "Ya tú eres hombre, ya te duermes, / mi amigo, ea . . ." ("You are already a man, you now go to sleep, my friend, hey . . . ") of the preceding stanza:

> No es verdad que tú seas hombre;
> eres un niño que no sueña.
> No es verdad que tú hayas sufrido:
> son cuentos tristes que te cuentan.

(It is not true that you are a man; you are a child who does not dream. It is not true that you have suffered: those are sad stories they tell you).

The second time they come toward the end of the poem, in the last stanza:

> La noche es bella, está desnuda,
> no tiene límites ni rejas.
> No es verdad que tú hayas sufrido,
> son cuentos tristes que te cuentan.
> Tú eres un niño que está triste,
> eres un niño que no sueña.

(Night is beautiful, it is naked, it has neither limits nor bars. It is not true that you have suffered, those are sad stories they tell you. You are a sad child, you are a child who does not dream.)

For Hierro the night is a positive value, almost a form of freedom; likewise, the reality of suffering is nothing but a fantasy, a sad story told to a child. When faced with reality Hierro tries to evade it, and, at most, remembers with nostalgic sadness a better world in a better time. Contrary to most of the social poets, Hierro does not react decidedly against the circumstance but turns away from it, only to dwell on the past or, still better, to move constantly from present to past, from concrete reality to dreams or fantasies.

While in Hierro the topic of the prisoner is related to childhood and lost innocence, de Nora's poem "La Cárcel" [Jail, *P.*, 124–27], published in *Espadaña*, follows very nearly Alonso's conception of all men as dead bodies whose flesh and blood are imprisoned, waiting for deliverance. Angela Figuera Aymerich conceives of prison as encompassing all the limitations imposed by a repressive society to all free men:

> Nací en la cárcel, hijos. Soy un preso de siempre.
> Mi padre ya fue un preso. Y el padre de mi padre.
> Y mi madre alumbraba, uno tras otro, presos,
> como una perra perros. Es la ley, según dicen.

(I was born in jail, my sons. I am forever a prisoner. My father was already a prisoner. And my father's father. And my mother gave birth to prisoners, one after the other, like the female dogs give birth to dogs. It is the law, so they say.)[8]

And, again, only the innocence of childhood knows freedom:

> Un día me vi libre. Con mis ojos anclados
> en el mágico asombro de las cosas cercanas,
> no veía los muros ni las largas cadenas
> que a través de los siglos me alcanzaban la carne.
>
> Mis pies iban ligeros. Pisaban hierba verde.
> Y era un tonto y reía
> porque en los duros bancos de la escuela
> podía pellizcar a los vecinos,
> jugar a cara o cruz y cazar moscas,
> mientras cuatro por siete eran veintiocho
> y era Madrid la capital de España
> y Cristo vino al mundo por salvarnos.

(One day I was free. With my eyes anchored on the magic wonder of the near things, I saw neither the walls nor the long chains that reached my flesh from beyond centuries. My feet moved lightly. They stepped on green grass. And I was dumb and laughed because I could pinch my classmates in the hard benches of the school, and play heads or tails and chase flies, while four multiplied by seven were twenty-eight and Madrid was the capital city of Spain and Christ came to the world to save us.)

This feeling of deception and oppression, represented by prison, the loss of innocence, and the yearning for a lost world, lies at the basis of the poetic rebellion that produced, during the 1950s, a committed social poetry in Spain. From 1944 to 1951—the year *Espadaña* was suppressed because of censorship problems—several texts opened the way for the new poetic awareness. Many well-known social poets were already moving in that direction. By the early 1950s, the social sensibility was established and political developments only helped its exterior manifestation in literature and social action.

Chapter Three
A Few Selected Poets

By 1951, Spain had entered a new period in her history; the 1940s had been a postwar period, with all its economic and political limitations, a period of total consolidation of the new regime. With the international recognition of Spain, strongly supported by the United States, the new decade was characterized by the definite conviction among the oppositional forces that the Spanish regime was to continue, invulnerable. But in spite of the growing industrialization of the country, the social and economic situations were still far from adequate. The year 1951 was marked by the first riots, and first general strike, in Barcelona and Madrid against economic injustices.[1] It was also the year of the first social books by Blas de Otero and Gabriel Celaya. The general mood had changed from passiveness to action.

In literature the 1940s had been years of prolific production, especially in poetry. There were many publications of all sorts; many were the poets, old and new, with little critical selectivity. It seems natural, then, that at the beginning of the new decade the need was felt to assess the previous decade's production, and to determine which were the new, authentic poets. This task was done by many, but it was Francisco Ribes who offered the best and most representative selection of new poets in his *Antología consultada de la joven poesía española* [Selected Anthology of the Young Spanish Poetry], published in 1952.

A Poll of Poets

In effect, Ribes prepared the anthology from the results of a poll of some sixty "personalities" he deemed best suited to answer with proficiency the following question: "Who are, in your opinion, the ten best poets alive today who became known during the last decade?" (*A.C.*, 10). The procedure seemed an adequate one to obtain a picture of preferences among a very specific group of readers.

The narrow selection of respondents indicates that the editor not only believed, as he put it in the prologue to his book, that poetry was not read by a great number of people, but also that it would remain an interest of a very limited group. It is significant that among the polled "personalities" are included all nine poets selected as the best ones to have appeared after the war. Poets read poets. None of the remaining names of the list included persons with intellectual interests outside literature, and more specifically, beyond poetry.

Starting from the observation that in Spain "the jungle of our poetic productions grows denser with every day, and the guides are so many and so daring that they are better in misguiding than in leading" (*A.C.*, 9), the editor hoped to offer to the general public—those who did not read poetry—an authoritative selection of what had been really good poetry in the first ten years after the war. This need for an edition to divulge poetry speaks of a situation that could explain the main tenet of the social poets—that is, to write poetry for the majority of people. Implied in this declaration is the fact that most of the poetry written in Spain during those years was alien to the general public.

The interest in the public has to be seen in light of the fast transformations of communications and mass media in postwar Spain. An important force in that direction was the government itself via its propaganda. Being a poet was an easy and rewarding activity in a country where magazines, literary prizes and collections, editorial houses, recitals, and anthologies were counted by the hundreds. With such a bounty of publishing facilities, any and every poet could enjoy the pleasure of seeing his name, and his flimsy sonnet, in print. The result of this practice was, obviously, a proliferation of unreadable poetry, and an ensuing lack of interest by much of the general public.

The *Antología consultada* tries to palliate this lack of editorial selectivity, although its editor is careful enough not to hurt anyone. The end result of the method does not necessarily produce a list of the best poets; it does give, however, a good idea of what the main aspects and interests of the Spanish poetic intelligentsia were at that particular time. Of the many names that appeared in the Spanish poetic world during the 1940s, the nine poets who received the highest percentage of nominations summarize the main trends of the decade and set the "two perfectly differentiated attitudes" vaguely alluded to by the editor. These are well represented in the commentaries provided by the poets themselves. Of particular interest for understanding the role of social poetry in Spain are the ideas about the reading public, the communicative value of poetry, and its content and style.

The Public

First and foremost among the differences is the problem of the reading public. Ribes allows that although poetry is not an art for everybody, it should not solely be for a "few initiated." He believes that "the poetry of each period always gathers the most peculiar vibrations of its moment and prefigures that of the immediate future" (*A.C.*, 8). This temporalist interpretation of the poetic phenomenon, although not new, seems to be in accordance with the practical value of poetry as understood by the social poet; but, a few lines later, another sentence introduces a quite different idea: that poetry "is perhaps the only possible refuge against the aggressive meanness of the circumstance" (*A.C.*, 8–9). These seemingly contradictory conceptions of poetry find perfect harmony not only in the mind of the editor, but also in that of some poets, for whom poetry claims the right to the highest spiritual experience.

For them, their readers cannot be but other singular souls, the selected few who have been educated and sensitized to poetic language and poetic experience. Rafael Morales puts it in these unequivocal terms:

> The great Vicente Aleixandre says that the poet who writes for himself is killing himself for lack of destiny. What an exact truth! I have always thought likewise and I have written, not for a minority, but for the majority of men. What I have just said does not mean that I simplify my poetry by falling into the easy and well-trodden way in order to make it reach everybody. That is what they do who do not know better. But, I always try to be understood, at least by a relative majority, that is, by the only majority upon which artists should count. Art has never been made for people with unrefined taste. (*A.C.*, 126)

The opposition between *majority* and *minority* is intentionally blurred by Morales, in what is a good example of how easy it was for many to defeat any intention of ideological confrontation. He is alluding to Otero's phrase "the vast majority," with which the latter, in turn, paraphrased the famous dedication by Juan Ramón Jiménez: "to the immense minority." Thus two opposing views on poetry, and the different basic attitudes by which they are supported, are shown in contrast. Jiménez was the representative of elitism in literature. A literary tradition, a period's sensibility, and surely a personal preference should be cited as factors affecting his attitude. In Morales's case there is no other tradition than the one invented by his contemporaries imitating neo-classical formalism. His being included later among the social poets speaks of the politics of literature during the postwar period.

After *Poemas del toro* [Poems of the Bull, 1943], a book of plainly insipid sonnets inspired by vaguely idealistic conceptions of Spain's spiritual values, Morales seemed to veer toward "rehumanization" with his book *Los desterrados* [The Exiled, 1947], in which his stilted versification tries to "beautify" in poetic terms the sad picture of human suffering. In spite of the title, there is no direct reference to Spanish reality in the book. A few verses from "Los ciegos" [The Blind Men] will suffice to give an idea of how Morales does not really perceive the subject of his poem, but only the poem itself, which he constructs as a summation of topical images, vocabulary, and conceptions, all quite far removed from any true rehumanization:

> Son sombra nada más, tan sólo sombra,
> nube de carne que en el suelo pesa;
> en su entraña el abismo, y en su frente
> un celeste silencio sin estrellas.

(They are shadows, only shadows, clouds of flesh that weigh on the floor; inside of them the abyss; and on their forehead a heavenly silence without stars.) (*A.C.,* 139)

For him, the different forms of human suffering—blindness, leprosy, madness—are merely motives for vacuous versifications in which, at the most, a charitable desire to feel compassion is evident. The mechanical quality of Morales's inspiration is further confirmed by his later evolution as a poet. His next two books, *Canción sobre el asfalto* [Song on the Asphalt, 1954] and *La máscara y los dientes* [The Mask and the Teeth, 1962], try to conform to the social poetry then in fashion. In the first book he takes as subjects of his formulaic poems the ugliest or most meager aspects of reality, only to mimic interest in their existence. What he really does is look at them from afar, touch them with the magic wand of his poetic inspiration—namely the ability to versify and use rhyming terms that sound somehow profound—and produce a seemingly emotive poem. If there is any real emotion, it is totally diluted in the process.

One of these poems appears in the *Antología consultada*, "Los traperos" [The Rag Collectors], in which the sad figures of these victims of social injustice are transformed into purely pictorial and mawkish caricatures of life's miseries:

> Y llevan en un saco los zapatos
> negros y fríos de un muchacho muerto,
> la muñeca sin brazos y sin ojos
> y un tímido abanico dieciochesco,
> mostrando en sus varillas solitarias
> el pequeño temblor de su esqueleto,
> comido de ratones donde puso
> antiguamente su rumor el viento.
> Un azulado traje de obrerita
> se pliega en un rincón donde el silencio
> íntimo y sucio pone su ternura
> entre la mansa lana y el recuerdo.

(And they carry in their bags the black and cold shoes of a dead lad, the doll without eyes or arms, and the timid lady's fan that shows in its lonely sticks the subtle tremor of its skeleton, eaten by rats that part where some time ago the wind touched it with its rumor. A bluish dress that belonged to a little working girl is folded in a corner where the silence, dirty and intimate, puts its tenderness among the tame wool and the remembrances.) (*A.C.*, 143)

A similar fondness for the sentimental is found in his later poems, where even regular versification has disappeared in imitation of a free, expressive poetry of social protest. For him poetry is mainly an exercise in rhetoric. When everyone was writing sonnets about serious matters such as love, country, and the spiritual superiority of Spain, the God-chosen land, Morales produced his sonnets to the bull. When the influence of tremendism was the norm, he versified in a similar way, and so on and so forth. Morales was not the only one to jump on the bandwagon; as a matter of fact, several poets went through a similar evolution, and perhaps this should be taken into consideration when assessing the true value of their production. That Morales was sincere in his own evolution as a poet matters little; what does matter is the fact that he dutifully followed an evolution that coincided with the main current of poetic expression in a particular period, although seemingly contrary to his own convictions. He stands now as an example of what happened in Spain between the end of the war and the subsequent slow weakening of a regime and its ideological basis.

The two groups of poets selected for the anthology that correspond to the "two perfectly differentiated attitudes" are formed by Carlos Bousoño, José María Valverde, and Vicente Gaos, representing the preference for classical meters and the more abstract and self-centered topics of religious, amorous, and philosophical poetry; and by Blas de Otero, Gabriel Celaya, and Eugenio de Nora, representing social poetry. José Hierro remains in a position of theoretical indecisiveness and should be set apart, although he is markedly inclined toward the social group.

None of the poets in the first group addressed the problem of the public, because their individualistic conception of poetry did not require that they consider the matter at all. At the most they fancied a possible coincidental spirit who will read their works as if they were an echo of his own soul. For them, the concept of minority— if at all present in their minds—must have been as exclusive as the one supported by Morales. Literature is an art form cultivated by highly cultured and sensitive persons for the enjoyment of other, identical, selected spirits. This conception is not at all inadequate; it corresponds with what has been the norm in matters of written poetry in Spain. In no period of modern history has the poet been read by more than a few interested people. Only the popular poet counts as his audience a larger and socially wider group.

The poets in the second group are less realistic in their understanding of the actual value of poetry in contemporary society; they dream with the idea of doing, to a certain extent, what the popular poet can do—to be heard and understood by a large number of men, and particularly by those who do not have a sophisticated poetic education. But this desire is not an easy one to satisfy; while they hope and strive for a wider audience, they are quite aware of the difficulties in reaching their aim. They differ from the poets of the first group in their willingness to make poetry available to all, in spite of the fact that poetry lacks readers.

Otero's attitude is typical of the social poet: "We are well aware of the difficulties in making ourselves heard by the majority of people. Also in this matter many are called and few are chosen. But let us start by calling the people, because I am almost certain that the cause of such lack of interest is more in the voice than in the ear" (*A.C.*, 174). By switching the deficiency in the poet-reader relationship from the reader to the poet, Otero opens the way for a revision of literary practices among poets. They cannot blame the public for its lack of interest in poetry, since it has been the poet's own inability to communicate interest which has been the cause of the public's disaffection.

Gabriel Celaya, adding a political overtone to the matter, takes a more radical position. What in Otero is only general and unspecific in Celaya becomes specific and socially meaningful; it shows a rather utopian vision of poetry: "And nothing seems as important in recent lyrical poetry as that abandonment [by the poet] of the minorities, and that constant search—against the semieducated petite bourgeoisie—for a contact with some social sectors that have been left unattended and are ringing urgently in our consciousness asking for life" (*A.C.*, 46). But even to assume that poetry has been the privilege of the bourgeoisie is giving it too much credit.

De Nora seems more realistic, as an experienced editor of *Espadaña*, of which he barely printed 250 copies of each issue. Commenting on the idea of the anthology, he writes: "I applaud with enthusiasm, my friend, in principle and without much knowledge of it, your initiative to do this 'poetic plebiscite.' It is a project that corresponds perfectly to what should be the life of poetry, and not in little magazines and little books of sickly minorities, not in scandalous deluxe editions to exhibit, but the object of interest and confrontation for large sectors" (*A.C.*, 156). Such an enthusiastic paragraph would be as utopian as Celaya's comment if it were not followed by these words: "I am sure you have been able to do very little, because I imagine your poll has not gone outside of the literary groups; but something is something; I hope the book reaches much farther."

Poetry as a Form of Communication

For Crémer, a poet who had been writing "committed" poetry from the mid-1940s, the public is a factor not yet determined. That there is to be an addressee appears evident from the conviction that poetry is communication. He writes: "Poetry is communication (Vicente Aleixandre). Then, there is nothing else to do but to discover the being to whom we address our message" (*A.C.,* 65). It is clear, then, that for him the poet has a message, a very definite matter to discuss, and a specific intellectual content to communicate to the rest of men.

His naming Aleixandre indicates that the poet of the Generation of 1927 had been influential in the development of new conceptions about poetry. In effect, knowing his situation as master of the new poets, Aleixandre had made his views on poetry explicit, thus offering a direction to follow. Reading his precepts from "Poesía, moral, público" [Poetry, Moral, Public], published in 1950,[2] helps to understand which were the principal points of debate among the Spanish poets at the turn of the decade. The title itself points toward a conception of poetry well aware of its social function.

In 1951, a few months after the release of "Poetry, Moral, Public," Aleixandre restated the main ideas in his article "Poesía, comunicación," [Poetry, Communication, *O.C.,* 1580–83], which definitively set the principle of poetry as a form of communication among men. This idea is related to his conception of the poet as able to contact different levels of reality and make them available—through his poetic powers—to others who are less endowed with an understanding of reality. Aleixandre does not mean that the poet is a superior being, aloof from the rest of humanity. On the contrary, "the poet is the man . . . in an intensified state." His work is a man's work: "Poetry starts in man and in man ends." This is the rehumanization the new poets were looking for. It establishes the basic communal character of poetry: "Poetry presupposes, at least, two men," but it strives for the community of all men: "All poetry is, in potence, multitudinous, or it is not at all."

The objective of poetry, then, is to establish lines of communication among men; consequently, "Poetry is not a matter of *ugliness* or *beauty,* but of *muteness* or *communication.*" If to this is added the idea that "all poetry carries with it a moral," it is easy to conclude that Aleixandre was in favor of the new development toward a literature committed to the betterment of man. But he does not necessarily endorse a specifically social poetry. All of the poets represented in the anthology supported the idea of poetry as a form of communication; but there are important differences between the meanings given to that conception among those in each of the groups already mentioned. While for the members of the first group the communicative value of poetry implies certain understanding of two germane—normally selected—spirits, for the social poets the communication implies in most cases a wide public sector. Except for Crémer, who is not very explicit about the matter, the other social poets are thinking in terms of a very concrete public: all of the people.

What to Communicate

Many subjects might be or become matter for literary communication. The foremost theorist of the communicative essence of poetry, Carlos Bousoño, says that the poet communicates only psychological contents, that is, a reality of his own: "Realist poetry? If you are referring with it to interior reality, I have no objections. All true poetry has always been realist poetry: there is no poet who does not transmit a *real* content of his soul (sensorial perception or fantastic intuitions, concepts and sentiments)" (*A.C.,* 25).[3]

Following this, Bousoño writes an individualistic and psychologically self-centered poetry; his poems deal mainly with the poet's personal interiorized experiences, be they religious, philosophical, patriotic, or amorous. Such is the case also with Vicente Gaos and, to a certain extent, with José María Valverde, who evolves differently in his work. Originally a member of the group of *Juventud creadora,* by the mid-1950s he had exchanged his self-centered interest in God and personal love for an altruistic interest in man and contemporary society. But his late evolution does not have the dramatic impact of Otero's own earlier transformation as a poet.

In his notes to the *Antología consultada,* entitled "Y así quisiera la obra" [And I Would Like My Work to Be Like This], Otero expresses this important change in his work: "Perhaps today more than ever it is necessary to write a poetry 'in accordance with the world.' But let it be understood that they should not permit anything negative or disoriented (I have to say it, even against my previous work)" (*A.C.,* 179). And further: "Task for today: to express a sense of brotherhood with the true tragedy, and then, as soon as possible, to try to overcome it" (*A.C.*, 179). From the self-centered poetry of interior problems, Otero moves to a world-centered poetry conceived as a task, with the specific duty to change things in the world.

The same is said, even more directly, by Celaya: "Poetry is not an aim in itself. Poetry is an instrument, among others, to transform the world" (*A.C.,* 44). Thus, what the poet has to communicate are all the human aspects related to man's life in society: "Nothing that is human must stay out of our work. In the poem there must be mud, and pardon me the very poetic poets. There must be ideas although the acephalic singers think otherwise. There must be in it the animal warmth. And there must be in it rhetoric, descriptions, and arguments, and even politics" (*A.C.,* 44). Celaya's words, so characteristic of his passionate involvement with ideas, are a complete program that was to be followed by many younger poets. But neither he nor Otero, de Nora, or Crémer is more specific about the kind of messages or contents the poet has to communicate; they leave room for a vast definition of the poet's duty, their central tenet being an enthusiastic belief in the power of poetry to affect the ways things change in the world.

The How of Communication

The social poets included in the *Antología consultada* have few ideas in relation to the best techniques of composition or the appropriate style to use when writing poetry to communicate with a vast majority of people. In general, they agree in condemning formalism and aestheticism for their inability to express and communicate the subjects of interest for the common man.

Celaya disregards the material part of poems as mere conduits for poetry which "passes through them as a current," and puts the poet into contact with the reader, creating a short circuit that "burns and reduces to nothing the verbal matter." De Nora is less radical in his appreciation of the poetic form: "I think that poetry should not be too brilliant; I myself, at least, look for conciseness" (*A.C.,* 154). Decorative beauty is, for him, a negative value because "the more the poet is preoccupied with 'beauty,' with 'form,' with 'poetry in itself,' the more he will separate himself from the essentially human life, both individual and social" (*A.C.,* 152). He has taken seriously Aleixandre's warning against aestheticism: "Woe to the poet that searches for beauty above all! Whoever wants to save beauty, he will lose it!"[4]

Celaya is equally opposed to the aesthetic ideal, as he categorically points to the differences between two types of poets: "The first ones are perfectionists, and they value in each poetic work its greater or lesser proximity to an absolute and fixed value they call Beauty. The others are temporalists and they only see in poetic works testimonies that, because they are human, are inseparable from here and now" (*A.C.*, 43). Naturally, he includes himself among the last ones. The antiaesthetic ideas of these writers lead them to a particular poetic style that, although not used exclusively in the social poem, is characteristic of it. Basic traits of this style are clarity of expression, simplicity in the exposition of ideas, and sincerity. This last aspect represents the moral equivalent of the rhetoric of direct communication. The need for sincerity—and consequently for the truth—is also part of Aleixandre's principles governing true poetry. In accordance with this, Crémer asks of the poet clear ideas and a good heart, two qualities he finds missing in the poets of his time. Otero requires from the social poet a real conviction about the subject: "I believe in social poetry, provided that the poet (the man) feels these themes with the same sincerity and the same strength with which he feels the traditional ones" (*A.C.*, 180). De Nora's request for conciseness and Celaya's proposition for an inclusion of all forms of linguistic expression in the poem give poetic validity to common, everyday language and to forms of narrative, oratory, discourse, and dialogue. None by itself nor all of them together determine the social character of a poem, but the tendency to equate them with social poetry has been the cause for misinterpretation of the real extent of the phenomenon in Spain.

A Form of Poetic Realism

Although in general Spanish poetry in the 1950s shows a series of common characteristics based on a temporalist interpretation of man, only a few poets wrote proper social poetry. The rest only touched similar subjects—Spain, everyday life, memories of boyhood, poverty—, used a similar style—simple language, colloquial tone, free verse—, and possibly wrote a few poems of protest or social awareness. But only those who believed in social change through political means, and used their poetic activity to lend a helping hand in the battle for a better society, are to be considered as fully social poets.

Still, as Vicente Aleixandre observes in *Algunos caracteres de la poesía española contemporánea* [Some Characteristics of Contemporary Spanish Poetry, 1955], the poetry of the period is fully centered on "human life in its historical dimension," which gives it a strong realist flavor conducive to a social interpretation of man's life and the world: "We seek to deduce that the new view of man as situated in the 'here' and a 'now' brings the consequence of a literary realism as the one seen today in Spain" (*O.C.*, 1435). It is in these general points of view and attitudes developed from the rehumanization of poetry that the social poets find an echo for their more specific commitment.

Chapter Four

The Preeminence of Blas de Otero

Although the *Antología Consultada* was not a collection of social poets, it should be considered as a manifesto of social poetry in Spain. Some poets included were developing, at that particular time, a conviction about the utility of poetry in the political and social life of the country. Their words about what they thought poetry was or should be are to be interpreted mostly as principles to be followed, and projects for future works, rather than as comments on their previous publications. This is particularly true in the case of Blas de Otero, who was to become the best-known representative of social poetry in Spain.

When the anthology appeared in 1952, the poems and books of social inspiration published in Spain were few. It is around that year, however, that the poets began to publish distinct social verses, perhaps hoping for a chance to alter the situation in a country that was suffering from some social unrest after more than ten years of strict political control by the government. Out of the authors selected for the anthology, de Nora, Crémer, and Celaya had already written some socially directed poetry; José Hierro had published a book seen as a comment on postwar Spain, but he did not continue this historical aspect of his work in subsequent books or develop a theory of poetry that could be called social. Blas de Otero, in turn, was known for his *Cántico espiritual* [Spiritual Song, 1942] and for two books that had produced favorable critical commentaries because of their "human" quality: *Angel fieramente humano* [Fiercely Human Angel, 1950] and *Redoble de conciencia* [Drumroll of Conscience, 1951].

The Rebel Angel

Dámaso Alonso was the critic who acclaimed Otero's book for the same reasons his own work, *Children of Wrath,* had been acclaimed in 1944: it expressed the "double anguish of which all of us were participants, the permanent and essential anguish in any man, and the particular one of these sad years of demolition, of catastrophic apocalypse."[1] In effect, *Angel fieramente humano* and *Redoble de conciencia* are very much like Alonso's book in that they express anguish and despair, and clamor to God in overdramatic tones. They were the works of an "uprooted" poet, as Alonso called those who had reacted strongly to their human situation in a chaotic world. But, contrary to the implicit recognition of man's dependence on God's supreme will in Alonso's book, Otero takes the stand of the rebel. He will assert man over God.

Born in 1916, Blas de Otero was twenty years old at the onset of the Civil War. Like many other young men of his day, he lived through the anguish of actual fighting and, once the war was over, had to contend with the psychological consequences of the ordeal. His first poems bespeak the spiritual union with God as a solution to human suffering. The poet hopes for individual satisfaction away from the immediate circumstance: "Dios me está preparando una morada / donde yo, nada más, me baste a mí" ("God is preparing a house for me where I, myself, will suffice in myself ").[2]

Many Spanish poets of the period had turned to God in search for a superior realm where they could find respite from their sufferings. Spain itself had become the land of a triumphant God, and religious values had been set as the highest level of importance, together with love of the motherland and her imperial tradition. It is quite probable that Otero soon realized that his monologue with a God who did not answer was nothing but a way of escaping from reality; it was a defense the State itself had insisted upon, knowing it was to act in its favor. Religion and politics were closely related; the seach for God was almost like another form of political commitment. Otero, then, left aside his religious preoccupations when he discovered the human, concrete reality behind all that spiritual anguish. His process of disenchantment with God, or better yet his realistic confrontation with man's problems, is seen in the consecutive titles *Angel fieramente humano* and *Redoble de conciencia.*

A first step into disillusionment seems to be his desperate discovery that God is silent, and that even his own words of prayer are only silence: "te voy llamando / a golpes de silencio" ("I am calling you with blows of silence").[3] A whole section of *Angel fieramente humano* devoted to desperate poems to God takes the title of the sonnet "Poderoso silencio" [Powerful Silence]: "¡Poderoso silencio con quien lucho / a voz en grito: grita hasta arrancarnos / la lengua, mudo Dios al que yo escucho!" ("Powerful silence with which I fight with screams: mute God to whom I listen, scream until our tongues are ripped out!" *H.I.M.*, 44). Calling God vainly the poet has lost his voice and hopes: "De tanto hablarle a Dios, se ha vuelto mudo / mi corazón." ("After so much talking to God my heart has become mute", *H.I.M.*, 67). And since this totally impassive God seems only to harm man, the poet wishes that He leave him alone, even to the point of wanting to kill God: "Déjame. ¡Si pudiese yo matarte, / como haces Tú, como haces Tú! ("Leave me alone! If I could kill You, as You do, as You do!" *H.I.M.*, 66). All men are equally the victims of an enigmatic and cruel God: "los que luchan contra Dios, deshechos / de un solo golpe en su tiniebla honda." ("the ones who fight against God, the ones that are destroyed by an only blow in their deep darkness," *H.I.M.*, 59).

Once he has reached such a level of desperation, the poet turns his eyes to life itself: "¡Quiero vivir, vivir, vivir!" ("I want to live, live, live!" *H.I.M.*, 68), and finally calls the rest of mankind, asking that they too free themselves—as he has done—from simulated and false transcendental needs: "¡Oh, sed, salid al día! / No sigáis siendo bestias disfrazadas / de ansia de Dios. Con ser hombres os basta." ("Oh, be alive, get out to the day! Stop being beasts that simulate the desire of God. Being man is enough," *H.I.M.*, 36). Reality appears to Otero as concrete, historic, and immediate: "Que cada uno aporte lo que sepa" ("May each one contribute what he knows," *H.I.M.*, 79). He records the last years of Spanish history and the poet's awareness of his fellow men:

> Ocurre, lo he visto con mis propios medios.
> Durante veinte años la brisa iba viento en popa,
> y se volvieron a ver sombreros de primavera
> y parecía que iba a volar la rosa.
>
> En 1939 llamaron a misa a los pobres hombres.

Se desinflaron unas cuantas bombas
y por la noche hubo fuegos japoneses en la bahía.
Estábamos—otra vez—en otra.

Después oí hablar en la habitación de al lado.
(Una majer desgañitada, loca.)
Lo demás, lo aprendisteis directamente.
Sabíamos de sobra.

(It happens, I have seen it with my own means. For twenty years the wind
flew freely, and again were seen spring hats and it looked as if the rose
was going to fly. In 1939 they called the poor men for Mass. A few bombs
were deflated and there were Japanese fires at night in the bay. We were—
again—in another one. Afterwards I heard somebody talking in the next
room. [A crazy woman, crying her voice out.] The rest, you have learned
it directly. We very well knew.)

That woman's voice in the next room awakens in the reader the
sensibility of human nearness and solidarity, aspects which are also
alluded to by the use of the first-person plural pronouns. An interrelation, a communication, between the people and the poet has
been established. It follows, then, that his poetic voice should be
directed to his fellow men: "Definitivamente cantaré para el hombre"
("I will definitely sing for man," *H.I.M.*, 35). That decision will
be expressed several times in Otero's work.

The Fallen Angel

The sweeping transformation of Otero's view on the world and
on his position in it as a man and a poet is definitive in 1955, with
the publication of *Pido la paz y la palabra* [I Ask for Peace and the
Right to Speak]. It is, precisely, one of the subjects of the book.
In "Juicio final" [Final Judgement," *H.I.M.*, 39–40], one of the
several compositions that deals with it, the speaker is the poet
himself explaining his conversion to the new understanding of man
in the world. There is a critical ring to his words, a tendency to
ridicule, without laughing, his previous views on man, which are
the views of many.

The poem is structured around ironical resonances from the Catholic prayer, "I Confess" (*Yo, pecador,* in Spanish), combined with
allusions to Otero's own previous books. The title in itself has a

religious as well as a political connotation, especially in those years of hasty final human judgments. For Otero it means the final recognition of man's intransigent materialism. The poet's confession is completely opposed to what the prayer requires from the speaker; he confesses his sinful human condition, but does not repent; in other words, he does not turn to God for mercy, but accepts fully his being a man among men. It is important to observe that the use of the same initial words of the prayer ("Yo, pecador, me confieso . . ."), assures the shocking effect upon a Catholic reader by its complete reversal of meaning:

> Yo, pecador, en fin, desesperado
> de sombras y de sueños: me confieso
> que soy un hombre en situación de hablaros
> de la vida. Pequé. No me arrepiento.

(I, a sinner, finally, desperate because of the shadows and dreams, I confess that I am a man in the situation of talking to you all about life. I sinned. I do not repent.)

Of no less notoriety is the fact that the speaker characterizes himself as a poet who has to talk about life to a second-person plural. From a monologue before God he has changed to a discourse to other men as their addressees. And if he speaks, it is because that is what he has to do. This element of obligation is also present in other social poets, because all coincide in having an ethically self-appointed poetic duty:

> Nací para narrar con estos labios
> que barrerá la muerte un día de estos,
> espléndidas caídas en picado
> del bello avión aquel de carne y hueso.

(I was born to narrate with these lips that one of these days will be erased by death, the splendid nosedives of that beautiful airplane of flesh and bones.)

In an allusion to his previous book, *Angel fieramente humano,* Otero touches a motive related to the idea of the fallen man as seen in other postwar poets. For him, though, the fall from heaven, or paradise, is not negative; it is something that man has brought upon himself when trying to reach beyond his human realm. Falling defines him as a man in a specific circumstance he assumes as his own:

Alas arriba disparó los brazos,
alardeando de tan alto invento;
plumas de níquel: escribid despacio.
Helas aquí, hincadas en el suelo.

Este es mi sitio. Mi terreno. Campo
de aterrizaje de mis ansias. Cielo
al revés. Es mi sitio y no lo cambio
por ninguno. Caí. No me arrepiento.

(He threw his arms wings up, boasting of such a high invention; nickel feathers: write slowly. Here they are, driven into the ground. This is my place. My land. Landing strip of my desires. Topsided heaven. It is my place and I do not change it for any other. I fell down. I do not repent.)

Man, the fallen angel—"airplane of flesh and bones"—does not need wings anymore; they have been transformed to writing quill pens that, "driven into the ground," serve for a better duty. The grounding is absolute. To reach to the "fatherland of man" one does not need wings: "Llegaré por mis pies . . . / a la patria del hombre." ("I will reach the fatherland of man . . . on my own feet.")

When this poem was published, Otero had been through a virtual spiritual conversion—he had embraced the Marxist ideology and had become openly opposed to the Spanish government and the society it had engendered. From then on his works were going to be devoted to his political and social commitments. Several of his compositions recount his conversion, possibly as an example of the appropriate conduct to be followed by those "converted" by his words. A text that expresses quite directly his attitudes and objectives appears in his book *En castellano* [In Plain Words], published in France, because of Spanish censorship, in 1959: "If now I change the subject, if I leave aside the paper and pen for the world and come out as new; if I get into the newspaper, it is only because I want to turn around the Gospel, because at last I have understood that it is better to save the world than to save my soul" (*H.I.M.*, 121). The moral issue is underlined by the reference to the biblical sentence, and by the last paragraph of the text: "I know the trick. But now, leaving aside the props and the trap, I get out of the soul and get into the sea, only to publicize with the example that I have already left unsaid with my papers" (*H.I.M.*, 121).

The Right to Speak

Otero's political commitment and his concentrated interest in Spain as a subject of his social poetry were partially responsible for the difficulties he had in publishing some of his books written after the release of *Ancia,* in 1958. For almost fifteen years the poet did not publish a new title in Spain. *Ancia*—a word created from the combination of *angel* and *conciencia,* first and last words of the titles of previous books—reordained the text of those two collections, adding a few new poems. Similarly, *Expresión y reunión* [Expression and Reunion, 1969] is an anthology of all his books, including the ones that appeared outside Spain: *En castellano, Este no es un libro* [This Is Not a Book, 1963], and *Que trata de España* [All About Spain, 1964]. After 1970 other books, mostly collections of old poems, appeared in Spain; for some time, however, before his death in June 1979, the poet had been silent.

The fact that for more than a decade the committed books could not be published in Spain indicates the pressures of censorship in Franco's Spain. It affected particularly the social poets who had to act themselves as censors of their own words. This limitation has been commented upon by Otero in a sentence like "Escribo y callo" ("I write and keep silent," *H.I.M.,* 107); and in references to the impossibility of saying what he has to say: "Digo . . . lo que me dejan" ("I say . . . what they allow me to say," *H.I.M.,* 110). This conflict of the poet becomes a topic, and is symbolized by the opposing terms voice/silence, light/darkness (day/night), truth/lie, expressions also used by other poets in a similar fashion. One way to fight oppression and censorship is by writing in a language that can be clear and easily understood by everyone, but that is also elusive and open to varying interpretations.

An excellent example of how Otero manages to create such language is an untitled poem from *Pido la paz y la palabra* that combines original images with straightforward language, literary allusions, and set symbols. The composition, written in very short verses that lighten the rhythm to a fast pace, starts with two brief unities in plain language, almost synonymous; the reiteration stresses the intimate relationship between "necessity" and "truth." "Ni una palabra / brotará / en mis labios / que no sea / verdad. / Ni una sílaba/ que no sea / necesaria." ("From my lips will never sprout a word that is not truth. Not a syllable that is not necessary," *H.I.M.,*

110–11). A section follows that develops a personal symbol of clear meaning: "Viví / para ver / el árbol / de las palabras, di / testimonio / del hombre, hoja a hoja." ("I lived to see the tree of words, I gave testimony of man, leaf by leaf," *H.I.M.*, 111). Among the literary allusions in the poem are two verses of an old romance ("Hoy no tengo una almena / que pueda decir mía") and other two from Fray Luis de León; in this last case the poet introduces a change, adding in the next verse something the original writer did not write, nor could have intended to: "Oh campo / oh monte, oh río / Darro . . . ("Oh countryside, oh mountain, oh river Darro").

Cases of subtle changes of common expressions are the image "Quemé las naves / del viento" ("I burned down the ships of the wind") and a few verses in which life and poetry are made the same, as is characteristic of the social poet who declares his total immersion in reality: "Mis días / están contados, / uno, / dos, / cuatro / libros borraron el olvido, / y paro de contar." ("My days are numbered, one, two, four books erased the forgetfulness and I stop counting," *H.I.M.*, 111). Two symbols constantly used by the poet in his allusive language when referring to the power of the people—the sea—and to freedom—the air—close the composition: "Oh aire, / oh mar perdidos. / Romped / contra mi verso, resonad / libres." ("Oh lost air, lost sea. Blow against my verse, resound freely," *H.I.M.*, 111).

But censorship cannot account for the fact that Otero did not write much. His complete works are few, and save for the use of prose in *Historias fingidas y verdaderas* [Fictional and True Stories, 1970], and for less regular metric forms, the books written after *Ancia* tend to repeat what he had done in *Pido la paz y la palabra*. Published in 1955, this title marks the highest point in the notoriety of social poetry in Spain; it remains, then, as the most significant of Otero's books from an historical point of view. Its thirty-four poems contain the motives, topics, and techniques that make his poetry very peculiar and characteristic. The title is significant and appropriate to express the objective of Otero's work. It is further developed in this untitled poem:

> Pido la paz y la palabra.
> Escribo
> en defensa del reino
> del hombre y su justicia. Pido

la paz
y la palabra. He dicho
"silencio,"
"sombra," "vacío,"
etc.
Digo
"del hombre y su justicia,"
"océano pacífico,"
lo que me dejan.
                    Pido
la paz y la palabra.

(I ask for peace and the right to speak. I write in defense of the kingdom of man and its justice. I ask for peace and the right to speak. I have said "silence," "shadow," "emptiness," etc. I say "of man and his justice," "Pacific Ocean," what they allow me to say. I ask for peace and the right to speak. (*H.I.M.*, 110)

In spite of its brevity, this composition contains the basic characteristic elements of Otero's production: the constant references to the function of the poet in contemporary unjust society and his obsession with the act of saying (writing); the related reference to censorship; the literary biography in the reference to his former literary inclinations; the allusive language; the many different types of reiterations; the particular use of versification.[4]

Metric Patterns

In the composition just cited, as in several others in the book, and in later collections, Otero has abandoned the fixed, regular meters of traditional versification, which he normally prefers; instead, he favors, in this case, a less strict metric structure, based mostly on the succession of short sentences that are broken down by several enjambements and long pauses in interior positions of the verse. This technique is a freer variation of Otero's peculiar system of traditional versification; he breaks the rhythmic patterns of regular verses in order to avoid the easy melodic discourse of the well-known stanzas. The raucous voice of the poet requires the vacillation and roughness of a broken rhythm:

Mis ojos hablarían si mis labios
enmudecieran. Ciego quedaría,

> y mi mano derecha seguiría
> hablando, hablando, hablando.

(If my lips become mute my eyes would talk. I would end up blind, and my right hand would keep on talking, talking, talking.)

The breaking of a regular pattern seems more dramatic in an otherwise regular composition; thus the continuous use of classical metric forms in combination with free verse. The effect is different from the normally irregular free verse in that the reader's expectations are shaken by the unexpected breakage in the regular flow of the commonly used verses. The emotional tone of the voice, the speaker's deeply anguished state of mind, the profoundly desperate view on reality, and the anger are all underlined by this technique.

The poem "Sobre esta piedra edificaré" [On this rock I will build, *H.I.M.*, 96] offers a combination of metric forms. The first stanza is fully regular, with four hendecasyllabic verses lacking in cases of enjambement or long interior pauses:

> Testigo soy de ti, tierra en los ojos,
> patria aprendida, línea de mis párpados,
> lóbrega letra que le entró con sangre
> a la caligrafía de mis labios.

(I am your witness, dust in my eyes, fatherland I have learned, line of my eyelids, terrible letter that was fixed with blood in my lips.)

The emotion is mostly centered in the linguistic allusions to common expressions: *Tener tierra en los ojos* ("to be blind to reality"), and *la letra con sangre entra* ("knowledge is achieved with pains"). The second stanza introduces two enjambements, a verse divided internally by two long pauses, and one shorter verse of only seven syllables. The tension in the voice is more noticeable, particularly in the last line:

> Y digo el gesto tuyo, doy detalles
> del rostro, los regalo
> amargamente al viento en estas hojas.
> Oh piedra hendida. Tú. Piedra de escándalo.

(And I say your gesture, I give details of your face, I give them sourly to the wind in these leaves of paper. Oh cut stone. You. Stone of scandal.)

The last stanza has six verses instead of four; of these, only one is hendecasyllabic; it also contains very violent enjambements in two verses with almost confusing repetitions of the same words and same syntactical pattern. A literary allusion that is sharply cut is unfinished, only to be modified by a totally unexpected word, which puts an end to the poem in a climax of emotional disturbance:

> Retrocedida España,
> agua sin vaso, cuando hay agua; vaso
> sin agua cuando hay sed. *"Dios, qué buen*
> *vasallo,*
> *si oviesse buen . . ."*
> Silencio.

(Backward Spain, water without a glass, when there is water; glass without water, when there is thirst. "God, such a god vassal if he had . . . " Silence.)

In some cases only free verse allows the poet all the expressive possibilities of a given utterance. The poem that begins with "Pido la paz y la palabra" is a good example of this requisite. The main sentence is written three different ways in the poem: first, as the complete initial verse, the second time it is broken into three verses, two of which are formed by additional elements; and at the end of the poem, it is divided into two verses. In each case the rhythm of the sentence is different and stresses different values of meaning, as if the poet were analyzing it for the reader; or better yet, as if the speaker were an orator who repeats the same sentence with varying intonations to make himself better understood by the public through the emotional reaction to the delivery of the speech. Repetition, with or without variation of the rhythmic, syntactic, or semantic patterns, is the normal procedure used by Otero in the composition of his poems.

Repetition and Resonance

It has been pointed out that poetic language is essentially reiterative.[5] In each poem, and in different periods of history, reiteration takes different forms. From, for instance, the parallelistic structure of the old Galaico-Portuguese lyrical song to the subtle repetitions of various kinds found in contemporary free verse, the amount of

variations is limited to certain basic patterns. Otero has a special
ear for repetition and uses it in many ways, offering what could be
a catalog of its possibilities.

The most common manifestation is the simple repetition of the
same word, phrase, or sentence in a poem, as in "Pido la paz y la
palabra," already commented upon. In certain cases the procedure
could become reiterative, as in the poem "Crecida" [Flood, *H.I.M.*,
38–40], from *Angel fieramente humano,* and other compositions in
which the repetition is almost obsessive:

> Con la sangre hasta la cintura, algunas veces
> con la sangre hasta el borde de la boca,
> voy
> avanzando
> lentamente, con la sangre hasta el borde de los labios
> algunas veces,
> voy
> avanzando sobre este viejo suelo, sobre
> la tierra hundida en sangre,
> voy
> avanzando lentamente, hundiendo los brazos
> en sangre,
> algunas
> veces tragando sangre,
> voy sobre Europa
> . . . .

(With blood up to my waist, sometimes with blood up to the rim of the
mouth, I walk forward slowly, with blood up to the rim of the lips
sometimes, I walk forward on this old soil, on the earth sunken in blood,
I walk forward slowly, sinking the arms in blood, sometimes swallowing
blood, I go over Europe)

This excerpt not only exemplifies the dramatic effectiveness of
the reiteration of a word, but also other forms of repetition common
in Otero's style, especially the anaphora. Normally this procedure
requires the repetition of the same word or words at the beginning
of several verses, sometimes even consecutive ones. In several compositions Otero follows this model; in some cases, though, he introduces effective changes, as in the example above, in which the
anaphoric repetition is transformed in mere reiteration by repeating
several times the same words in different positions inside the verses.

Another subtle variety of the technique consists in dividing the members of the repeated phrase and using them at the beginning of two consecutive verses, thus augmenting the number of anaphoras in the poem. Most commonly, and in keeping with old models of structuralization by anaphoric and parallelistic method, Otero repeats the same verse, or part of it, at intervals in a poem to indicate different sections, creating sometimes a parallel repetition very much like traditional songs. The poem "Vencer juntos" [To Win Together, *H.I.M.*, 106–7) begins with the following verses: "A las puertas del mundo. / Estoy llamando al día con las manos mojadas / a las puertas del mundo, mientras crece la sangre." ("At the doors of the world. I am calling the day with my hands wet, at the doors of the world, while the blood grows"). The anaphora reappears in verses eight and nine: "A las puertas del mundo estoy llamando, / mientras la sangre avanza" ("At the doors of the world I am calling, while the blood moves in"); and, somewhat reduced, is repeated again in verses fifteen and sixteen: "Doy con los labios en la aurora, llamo / a las puertas del mundo" ("I touch the dawn with my lips, I call at the doors of the world").

In general he tries to avoid the totally regular construction, as he does with regular versification, the reasons being that the poet does not want to reproduce already-known models, but rather to make the best of them by instilling new expressive values in the old formula. Repetition in itself works as a rhythmic pattern, that is, its effectiveness is based upon the recognition of relationships between two or more elements separated from each other in time. The recognition can be seen as a true resonance of the repeated element. It is in this resonance, or recognition by the reader, in which Otero is interested. By intensifying the effects of resonance the poet enriches the emotive communication of his language, going a step forward from the less concentrated repetitiveness of traditional lyrics.

The effects of resonance are obtained in the text not only by the kind of repetitions already commented upon, but also by acoustic procedures that combine themselves with semantic resonance. That is the case, for instance, with the slightly imperfect repetitions. In a reduplication, in a case of parallelism, or in an anaphoric poem, the repetition does not reproduce exactly the main member, but varies it in different ways; it either changes it lexically, keeping only an acoustic similarity: "Esta / es mi casa / . . . . Esta / es mi patria" ("This is my home . . . This is my fatherland," *H.I.M.*,

123), or changes it altogether, keeping only few basic repeated elements to allow the recognition of a tight relationship among two or more elements. This procedure proposes to the reader a creative reading not lacking in surprises.

In "Litografía de la cometa" [Lithograph of the Kite, *H.I.M.,* 154], the initial verses are the basis for repetitions with changes: "Otra vez / debo decir he visto estoy cansado / de ver / herrumbre añil enjalbegada roña." ("Again I must say I have seen I am tired of seeing blue rust and whitewashed filth"). Two stanzas—one at the middle of the poem, the other at the end—resound as very similar among themselves: "Otra vez / tienes tierra palabra / herramienta valor para enterrar un niño." ("Again you have earth word tool valor to bury a kid"), and "Otra vez / tienes tierra postura / andrajos de color para enterrar un niño." ("Again you have earth position colorful rags to bury a kid").

In a similar way, allusions of different kinds function as resonances. An old practice well known by poets, allusions allow for many and complex interrelations. Otero uses them sparingly. References to his own work are not rare, but the most abundant are the literary allusions. In *Pido la paz y la palabra* the author's allusions are several, from classic ones—"entrad / a pie desnudo en el arroyo claro / fuente serena de la libertad" ("with naked feet get into the clear brook, the serene spring of liberty," *H.I.M.,* 112), to Miguel Hernández—"Vientos del pueblo / esculpieron su mágica estatura" ("Winds of the people sculptured its magic height," *H.I.M.,* 106)— and César Vallejo—"España, espina de mi alma. Uña / y carne de mi alma. Arráncame / tu cáliz de las manos." ("Spain, thorn of my heart. Nail and flesh of my heart. Take your cup away from my hands," *H.I.M.,* 105).

The last example also offers another type of allusion that characterizes the tone of the poet's voice; it is related to the common or everyday language of the people. The common expression is slightly changed in ways similar to the changes effected in the case of repetitions. The resonance of a well-known expression that contains innumerable cultural elements impossible to name one by one, is much more than just a recognition: there is a renovated view of the well-established, an enlightenment of the commonly accepted, a sudden and surprising realization of a different possibility inside of the otherwise static reality as perceived every day.

The Language of the Immense Majority

The language of the poet—and in final terms his whole style—is largely dependent on his objectives, which, in turn, are dependent on the circumstances in which the poet finds himself. As said before, Otero's first reaction to the Spanish circumstances of the 1940s was to turn toward God, to an existentialist anguish. He soon realized the full extent of his predicament, and consequently changed his view on the world and on his objectives as a poet. Once he discovered that human sufferings were largely due to the unjust conditions in which large sections of humanity were living, and more so, that all humanity was condemned by its own meanness, he conceived his duty as a poet to inform others about the real situation they were living in, and to try, later, to create a better world: "Task for today: to demonstrate the sense of brotherhood with the living tragedy, and then, as soon as possible, to try to overcome it."[6] In both cases he had to address his fellow men, those who could benefit from his words, the vast majority of the common people who live under the oppression of a few, unaware of their true problems and of the possible solutions. It is very significant, then, that the phrase "the immense majority" appears many times in Otero's works.

The expression finds its origins in an epigraph to *Angel fieramente humano,* taken from Rubén Darío, a poet to whom Otero refers on several occasions: "I am not a poet for the majority of people; but I know that unfailingly, I have to go to them." A year after, a poem from his new book, *Redoble de concienca,* takes as its subject the poet's desire to make his word useful to his fellow man. The poem opens with the expression that will become a characteristic feature of social poetry:

> Es a la inmensa mayoría, fronda
> de turbias frentes y sufrientes pechos,
> a los que luchan contra Dios, deshechos
> de un solo golpe en su tiniebla honda,
>
> A ti, y a ti, y a ti, tapia redonda
> de un sol con sed, famélicos barbechos,
> a todos, oh sí, a todos van, derechos,
> estos poemas hechos carne y ronda.

(It is to the vast majority, foliage of dark foreheads and suffering chests, to these who fight against God, and are destroyed by a single blow in their deep darkness. To you, and to you, and to you, round fence of a thirsty sun, unenriched seedlings, to all of you, oh, yes, to all are directed these poems made of flesh and song.) (*H.I.M.,* 59)

Man is seen as a victim of a cruel God; the poet is suffering the same as the rest of men, and offers his word of help, but with little certainty about how it will be of service. There is a deep sense of incompetence and even impotence in the last two stanzas of the sonnet:

> Oídlos cual al mar. Muerden la mano.
> de quien la pasa por su hirviente lomo.
> Restalla al margen su bramar cercano,
>
> y se derrumban como un mar de plomo.
> ¡Ay, ese ángel fieramente humano
> corre a salvaros, y no sabe cómo!

(Listen to them as if they were the sea. They bite the hand of whoever caresses their boiling backs. Their near roar strikes aside and they collapse like a leaden sea. Alas, that fiercely human angel runs to your aid, but it does not know how to save you!)

Otero expresses in this poem his belief in the function of the poet as an active member of society; for him this realization has come from his love and compassion for humanity. It is in his next book, *Pido la paz y la palabra,* where he definitively reaches a clear conviction, as shown by the first and last poems of the collection. "A la inmensa mayoría" [To the Immense Majority], published previously in the *Antología consultada,* opens the book and serves as an example of Otero's style at the moment when he purposely focuses his attention on the present historical and social circumstances of man, rather than on an existentialist view of humanity before a silent God.

The first stanza of the poem—four hendecasyllables rhymed in assonance—contains two enjambements and several interior pauses, thus breaking the rhythmic pattern of the classical form. The roughness of the voice and its spoken, or dramatic, character are also stressed by the apostrophic attitude present in the first verse, and underlined by the adverb, that points to the realistic "here" and "now" so important to the effect of immediacy akin to social verse:

> Aquí tenéis, en canto y alma, al hombre
> aquel que amó, vivió, murió por dentro
> y un buen día bajó a la calle: entonces
> comprendió: y rompió todos sus versos.

(Here you have, in song and soul, the man who loved, lived, died inside of himself and a good day went down to the street: then he understood: and he tore apart all his verses.) (*H.I.M.*, 91)

It is not surprising that the "fiercely human angel" has suffered a transformation, becoming a man—in a sense, the Messiah of a new religion. Only knowing that Otero writes with many and very subtle allusions allows the reader to understand the first stanza as a paraphrase of Christ's life summarized and as a resonance of the *Credo*. The title of another poem of the same book leaves no doubt about Otero's intentions: "On this rock I will build." The social prophet comes to change things for everybody, and consequently everybody is the destined recipient of his message.

From this introductory poem to the last one in the book—"En la inmensa mayoría" [In the Immense Majority]—there is an evolution. First came the will to be of help for all men, and finally the certainty that he, as a poet, belongs to that immense majority, is part of the totality of men. In strictly concise language Otero expresses the strength and enthusiasm he has acquired through his new faith:

> Podrá faltarme el aire,
> el agua,
> el pan,
> sé que me faltarán.
>
> El aire, que no es de nadie.
> El agua, que es del sediento.
> El pan . . . Sé que me faltarán.
>
> La fe, jamás.

(I could be denied the air, the water, the bread, I know they will be denied to me. The air, that does not belong to anybody. The water, that belongs to the thirsty. The bread . . . I know they will be denied to me. Faith, never.) (*H.I.M.*, 115)

In future works the topic of the "immense majority" continues to be present; no important change is recorded. In 1962, the editorial house Losada published in Argentina an edition of Otero's four books—*Angel fieramente humano, Pido la paz y la palabra, Redoble de conciencia,* and *En castellano*—under the general title of *Hacia la inmensa mayoría* [Toward the Immense Majority]. The same phrase is repeated or alluded to six times in *Que trata de España* [That Deals with Spain, 1964]. In one case, it appears as part of a poem listing the books written by the poet. In this particular case, the phrase is limited in its meaning to only the "lower people" of Spain:

> hablo
> para la inmensa mayoría, pueblo
> roto y quemado bajo el sol,
> hambriento, analfabeto
> en su sabiduría milenaria,
> "español
> de pura bestia," hospitalario y bueno
> como el pan que le falta
> y el aire que no sabe lo que ocurre.

(I speak to the immense majority, a people broken down and scorched by the sun, a hungry and illiterate people with a millenary wisdom, "the purely bestial Spaniard," hospitable and good as the bread he lacks, and the air that does not know what happens.)[7]

This identification of the majority with the lower class or the less educated is further insisted upon in a whole section of the book, entitled "Cantares" [Songs]. In it, popular songs are not only taken as models, but are also considered the only true poems, as the citation of Agusto Ferrán says: ". . . I have included a few popular songs . . . , to be sure that at least there will be something of value in this book" (*Q.T.E.,* 67). A short song pays tribute to the late poet Miguel Hernández and stresses the popular inspiration of Otero's work:

> La vela de mi barca
> tiene un remiendo.
> Navegaré con el
> viento del pueblo

(The sail on my boat has a patch. I will sail with the wind of the people.)
(*Q.T.E.*, 69)

It appears an inconsistency to say that the poet writes for the "immense majority" and then adds that the majority is illiterate; everybody knows that the lower classes do not read poetry; aside from the popular lyrics transmitted orally, they do not care about the literary type. Otero solves this problem in "C.L.I.M." (*Q.T.E.*, 58), a title that, he explains, means precisely "Con la inmensa mayoría" [With the Immense Majority]:

> Pedro Lorenzana bate el zapapico.
> Justo Corral hiende la perforadora.
> Talan con la pala del hacha Andrés, Nico.
> Atruena el taller la martilladora.
> Muchos (miles) siegan a golpe de hoz,
> ¿todavía?, el trigo que otros (tres) ahelean.
> *Soy sólo poeta:* levanto mi voz
> en ellos, con ellos. Aunque no me lean.

(Pedro Lorenzana beats the pick-axe. Justo Corral uses the drill. Andrés, Nico cut shrubberies with the axe. The mechanic's hammer resounds in the shop. Many (thousands) harvest with the scythe, still? the wheat that others (three) make bitter. *I am only a poet:* I raise my voice in them, with them. Even though they do not read my works.)

And as if the poem were not clear enough, Otero precedes it with this paragraph: "In the conditions of our hemisphere, literature is not for the majority because of the number of readers, but because of its subject." In simple terms, Otero does not concern himself anymore with the possible effectiveness of his work. "Voz del mar, voz del libro" ("Voice of the sea, voice of the book," *Q.T.E.*, 61–62), and "El mar suelta un párrafo sobre la inmensa mayoría" ("The sea says some words about the immense majority," *Q.T.E.*, 63), transform the same rationalization into very obvious poetic images; the sea symbolizes the people.

In still another poem titled "En la inmensa mayoría (1960)" [In the Immense Majority (1960), *Q.T.E.*, 174], the phrase acquires a wider meaning, becoming the vast variety of experiences of the world gained by the poet in his travels in Russia and China: ". . . no me podrán quitar la fe / en la inmensa mayoría / de todo

lo que ví, pisé, palpé / desde el Nevá nevado hasta Pekín." ("They
will not be able to take away from me my faith in the immense
majority of all I saw, I stepped upon, I touched, from the snow-
covered Neva to Peking") The Socialist ideology—others will talk
of political propaganda—is quite visible in these poems; after all,
they were published in Cuba and France, and only a few selections
of the book appeared in Spain before 1977.

The Autobiography of the Poet

As an ideologically inspired poet, Otero is an excellent example
of a socially committed writer in the contemporary non-Socialist
world. No other postwar Spanish poet living in Spain has been so
explicit about his political commitment in his work. Little inclined
to theorization, Otero has not written at any length in prose about
his conceptions of poetry; but preoccupation with the nature and
function of poetry is one of the main motives of his work. It should
be noticed, also, that most of those considered social poets tend to
elaborate the same motive in their poetry, making of it a topic
characteristic of the kind of literature they write.

It seems only natural that a poet who has taken as his main task
the writing of socially functional poetry in a country totally opposed
ideologically to a poetry so conceived (although quite aware of the
social or political function of literature, as attested by the subsidizing
of publications, and by censorship) will have to be overconscious
of his literary activity. But even so, when compared with other
Socialist poets, like Pablo Neruda, for instance, to whom he owes
much, Otero's poetry seems obsessively centered in the creative
process itself. It would not be totally inexact to say that he writes
mostly *about* social poetry, rather than writing social poetry itself.

Otero's preoccupation with the act of writing is not the result
of his Socialist ideas; rather it is the other way around. In his first
books it is quite evident that the poet becomes the central figure
of interest. Both *Angel fieramente humano* and *Redoble de conciencia*
document the personal evolution of the speaker as a poet, as a man
not only faced with his human destiny but with his being a poet,
a speaker among listening men. The rest of his books continue in
the same direction, making Otero's work a true biography of a poet;
from one stage to another, he moves on, talking about what he has
written, what he writes, and what he wants to write in the future.

His poetry concerns being a poet in a particular place at a particular time:

> Esta tierra, este tiempo, esta espantosa podredumbre
> que me acompaña desde que nací
> (porque soy hijo de una patria triste
> y hermosa como un sueño de piedra y sol; de un tiempo
> amargo como el poso
> de la historia)

(This land, this time, this frightening putrefaction that accompanies me since I was born [because I am the son of a sad motherland, a motherland as beautiful as a dream of stone and sun; son of a time bitter as the sediment of history] (*H.I.M.*, 104)

His historical determination explains, for him, the absolute necessity to become a social poet. But being an essentially lyric poet, his treatment of the social theme cannot help but be related to his own feelings and intimate experiences of the world. He is not the civic poet, but the voice of a people and their hopes as individuals in society. Consequently, he makes out of his own biography the central motive of his writing; in it are expressed and made manifest the main forces that originate an altruistic song for justice and happiness in the world.

Chapter Five

The Rhetoric of Communication in Gabriel Celaya

By 1952, the year of the publication of the *Antología consultada,* Gabriel Celaya was already known among the new poets intently writing a rehumanized poetry. In previous years he had published extensively, and had been very active in the new literary life of his country. His name was soon to become synonymous with social poetry and the theory of poetry as communication; he not only wrote for the *Antología consultada* the most direct comment in favor of a socially and politically committed literature, but he also grew personally involved in the social fighting of the day. In that same year, 1952, he released a clearly programmatic book, *Lo demás es silencio* [The Rest Is Silence], to be followed in subsequent years by several other collections as openly committed and equally accepted by the Spanish public as the voice of their subdued protest.

Endowed with a great facility for verbalizing, yet with practically no critical judgment for selectiveness, Celaya has produced huge amounts of verse and prose texts. Not all of what he has written is socially inspired; his social poems are relatively few, since his dedication to this particular kind of literature was limited mainly to a period of a few years—from approximately 1952 to 1962— roughly coinciding with the period of concern for the social aspects of literature among critics and public. A later editorial interest for social literature accounts for some new editions of Celaya's political verse in the 1970s, while the poet experiments with the newest fads in literary production.[1]

An Illustrative Biography

Although born in 1911, Celaya was not well known as a writer until the mid-1940s, when he founded a publishing house for poetry in San Sebastián, where he printed some of his many volumes of poetry and prose. This definitive move in his life has to be understood from his personal point of view, as well as from the particular Spanish political situation at the time.

Celaya, whose real name is Rafael Gabriel Múgica Celaya, had been interested in literature since his early youth; he even had frequented the literary circles of Madrid during the highly creative years of the Second Republic. After graduating from the School of Engineering in Madrid, he returned to San Sebastián to work for his family's company, seemingly choosing a business career. But, in spite of his family's disapproval, he published a book of poems. A second, unpublished collection won him a national prize, which helped Celaya decide to leave his job, move to Madrid, and become a full-time writer. Unfortunately, the war interrupted his budding literary career that same year, and for several more years to come he did not reinitiate his attempts at writing based on a matter of principle: "in the early 1940s the intellectuals surviving in the Peninsula thought that our correct attitude was to abstain from publishing as long as the situation did not change."[2]

The importance of these biographical details will be evident to anyone who considers carefully the tremendous intellectual, social, and political changes brought about by the Civil War. That Celaya's Basque family was probably inclined toward the political right wing does not imply that the young student in Madrid had to follow the same inclination. Those were years of social reform, of leftist ideals that affected intellectually and emotionally many writers and professionals who, later, would be seen in different parts of the world as exiled liberals. The impression made on the world by innumerable Spaniards who had to leave their country for their personal security, or for matters of principle, has obscured for many observers the fact that in Spain—the postwar Spain of Falange and Francoism—there were many more liberals who did not leave after the defeat of the Republic, who had to pretend to be in agreement with a political, social, and ideological system they could not confront, much less defeat. For these men, used to the intellectual freedom enjoyed during the period prior to the war, the ensuing years of forced silence must have been a difficult trial.

Gabriel Celaya was one of those who remained behind and lived what has been termed an "internal exile." The years 1938 to 1946 were for him the equivalent to an exile. While working for his family's firm he continued writing, but without active participation in the literary life of the country. Depression and illness, caused in part by the unbearable tension of being torn between hope and disillusion, brought him to the extreme of a total breakdown. The fact that his recovering meant breaking with the regimented world of a middle-class Basque industrialist shows that his problem had been related, to a great extent, to his social circumstances. The experiences of the ensuing years of regained freedom are important to his later development as a writer. His case is perhaps the best example of the strong influence of the particular political situation in Franco Spain over the evolution of postwar poetry from an existential fixation with personal destiny to a Socialist belief in poetry as a "weapon loaded with future," as Celaya himself states in one of his poems.

In the case of Celaya, literary history mingles with political history. Although it can be said that he was an aesthetically questionable poet, it cannot be denied that he aided in the evolution of Spanish poetry from an obsessive self-compliance to a sincere reformist commitment not only in Spain's tightly enclosed literary world, but also in the sphere of daily encounters with a rich and puzzling human reality. But there should be no doubt that Celaya's was not the kind of poetic voice which could have made social verse a memorable literary accomplishment. Others were better endowed for that effect, and definitely did a better job. Even before turning to social poetry, Celaya had written enough and experimented with other aesthetics to make clear that the defects marring his committed literature were not necessarily a result of limitations of that particular kind of poetry, as many critics of social or political lyrics would like to believe.

Some, perhaps the most outstanding, of Celaya's weaknesses are visible already in his early works written before the war. Impressed by the surrealist wave that touched the most important writers of prewar Spain, he wrote during his university years a first collection, *Marea del silencio* [Tide of Silence, 1935], which, besides its extremely imitative character, lacks essential understanding of surrealism. The poet is clearly thinking in verse, a characteristic that will define most of Celaya's poetic errors. Out of the many poems he wrote after the war, still before reaching a truly social commitment, those signed under the pseudonym of Juan de Leceta should be taken into consideration as forerunners of a particular style.

Juan de Leceta

Following closely the developments of Spanish verse after the war, Celaya despised the empty formalism of the officially accepted poetry, embracing the style and preferences of the existentialist poets, who were trying to express the sense of deprivation and personal anguish felt during that period. Commenting about the new developments in poetry, Celaya wrote in 1947: "Today, in an open and healthy reaction against the pretty and empty words of 'garcilasism,' the poets are looking for a substantially human poetry, brimming with properly felt truth and written in a vivid and piercing language."[3] The same year he published, under the pseudonym Juan de Leceta, *Tranquilamente hablando* [Talking Quietly], a book that represented very well the new trend. Under the same name appeared other compositions in *Espadaña,* and a long monologue in verse, *Las cosas como son* [Things as They Are, 1949]. All these compositions form a unity characterized by the persona of the speaker, the same in each one of them.

In effect, Juan de Leceta possesses a very distinct voice and a particular view of the world. That both are properly Celaya's does not take away from the speaker's own individuality. The pseudonym, used for obvious personal reasons at the time, became the name of a character representative of a transitional period in Celaya's personal evolution. Juan de Leceta is the poet who looks at reality pessimistically and ironically; he is the man who accepts his predicament because it is the only existence he knows, as all humans are equally condemned to the same destiny.

Once Celaya evolves from these negative ideas toward increased hope in human abilities to transcend materialistic circumstances, he can view Juan de Leceta as another, although not a totally different, entity. Thus, in *Las Cartas boca arriba* [Showing One's Cards, 1951], a book of letters to different friends, the last composition is addressed to Leceta, as if he were another living poet, friend of the author. Even in the introduction to *Las Cosas como son* Celaya

has already given Leceta a certain autonomy, although the title of
the note—"Digo, dice Juan de Leceta" [I Say, Leceta Says]—points
to the identification of both speakers. Several years later the poem
"La pistola en el pecho" [The Pistol in the Chest][4] is introduced as
written "from Juan de Leceta to Gabriel Celaya." Furthermore, in
1961, the poetry series Colliure, which published important books
of "social poetry," offered a volume titled Los poemas de Juan de Leceta
[The Poems of Juan de Leceta]. Included in this edition were Avisos,
Tranquilamente hablando, and Las cosas como son.[5]

The first two titles are collections of short poems written in direct,
conversational language. The combination of mostly heptasyllabic
meters in various strophic variations stresses a regular rhythmic
pattern and creates an effect of resonance of a long tradition of
sententious and critical poetry. The voice of the speaker sounds very
convincing because of its disdainful and ironic tone, akin to an
attitude of superior understanding of life's incoherences. The third
title corresponds to a long poem, a monologue in irregular stanzas
with a combination of regular meters, a rather repetitious and shapeless summation of just a few ideas: life does not make sense, but
it is beautiful, despite its imperfections; man is mortal and life is
his only possession.

Leceta appears as a shallow philosopher, preoccupied with death,
sensuality, and concrete reality. His sensibility is as blunt as his
intellectual acuteness; consequently, his poetry offers a rather dis-
appointing reading. Even the metric sameness of an almost equal
basic rhythm adds another shortcoming in the aesthetic failure of
this caricaturesque poetic persona who is unable to distinguish between different levels of meaning and different tones of voice. Leceta's poems are not properly social in inspiration. What makes
them interesting for the historian of social poetry is, more than
anything else, the speaker's observations about concrete reality and
the language in which they are couched. Juan de Leceta is a true
materialist, a firm believer in life, common, everyday life; his vocabulary, then, is that of conversation, the direct form of speech
that any man will understand. Far from his words any form of poetic
rhetoric, or of literary and subtle diction: "No quisiera hacer versos; /
quisiera solamente contar lo que me pasa." ("I would like not to
make verses; I would like only to tell what is happening to me,"
O.C., 284), and: "digo lo que quiero, y / sé que con decirlo sen-

cillamente acierto." ("I say what I want, and I know that by saying it simply, I do right," *O.C.*, 284).

The simplified expression was selected by Celaya with a clear purpose: "It seemed to me that to tune down the language, to talk about what everybody talks about in the street and to use, if it were necessary, a surprisingly direct and conversational language could save poetry from the isolation in which it was because of its talking about the clouds instead of dealing with what worries and interests everybody."[6] But he rarely was able to use such simplified language as he had used in the Leceta poems. Besides the direct language, in a few cases Juan de Leceta touches on themes or topics that could be considered social in nature. The most important in the context of the poetry of the day is his interpretation of God as the totality of men. Otero evolves from a mystic obsession with God to a form of communal religion of man; Celaya, in turn, touches the religious aspect, devoiding it of any serious theological implication. With his typical simple-mindedness he writes: "No hay duda de que tengo un temperamento religioso" [There is no doubt that I have a religious temperament, *P.C.*, 300], a poem in which he comments very bluntly on the abundant religious poetry of the period: "¡Señor, ya no resisto. / ¡Señor!, me siento roto. / ("Senor" no tiene nombre, / es un simple pretexto / para alargar dos puntos de admiración vacía)" ("Oh Lord!, I cannot resist any longer. Oh Lord!, I feel as if I were broken into pieces." ["Lord" has no name, it is a simple pretext in order to lengthen two empty exclamation points]).

The emptiness of the word "Lord" represented by the lack of a name is further commented upon in the poem: ("Señor" debería ser un tú, ser humano) (" 'Lord' should be a you, a human being"). This possibility is finally made effective in the last verse: "a todo el mundo llamo 'Señor' humildemente" ("Humbly I call everybody 'Lord' "). The same idea is repeated in *Las cosas como son,* except that the others are limited to the poet's friends; "y al pensar en Dios (¡no puedo evitarlo!) / pienso siempre en ellos." ("and when I think of God [I cannot avoid doing it!] I think always of them," *P.C.,* 325). The affirmation of man as the center of interest above God is not only a social topic, but an important statement in Franco's Spain, because it points to one of the strongest aspects in the political and ideological control of the people by the government. But Celaya's poem could very easily be interpreted from a Catholic point of view, without finding more than a slightly disturbing detail.

The attack on religion and the Church will always be very subtle among the Spanish social poets, perhaps because of the deeply rooted religious ideas and sentiments in their intended audience, the Spanish people, and certainly because of the powerful influence of the Church in the business of the country.

Other evident examples of social themes in Leceta's poems include two narrative compositions treating the life of the poor— "La mala vida que uno lleva" [The Difficult Life One Has to Bear] and "Cosas que pasan" [Things That Happen]; a short poem painting the materialistic bourgeoisie—"A todo tren" [In Full Swing]; another short composition relating the confrontation of the middle-class poet with the unjustly treated workmen—"A vuestro servicio" [At Your Service]; and "Todas las mañanas cuando leo el periódico" [Every Morning, When I Read the Newspaper], a poem that summarizes the conflict of Juan de Leceta in his relation to the world. A resolution of this conflict will take Celaya into the political activism of social poetry:

> Me asomo a mi agujero pequeñito.
> Fuera suena el mundo, sus números, su prisa,
> sus furias que dan a una su zumba y su lamento.
> Y escucho. No lo entiendo.
>
> Los hombres amarillos, los negros o los blancos,
> la Bolsa, las escuadras, los partidos, la guerra:
> largas filas de hombres cayendo de uno en uno.
> Los cuento. No lo entiendo.
>
> Levantan sus banderas, sus sonrisas, sus dientes,
> sus tanques, su avaricia, sus cálculos, sus vientres
> y una belleza ofrece su sexo a la violencia.
> Le veo. No lo creo.
>
> Yo tengo mi agujero oscuro y calentito.
> Si miro hacia lo alto, veo un poco de cielo.
> Puedo dormir, comer, soñar con Dios, rascarme.
> El resto no lo entiendo.

(I take a peek from my little hole. Outside the world whirls with its numbers, its hurry, its ires that make at once their jokes and cries. And I listen without understanding. The yellow men, the blacks or the white men, the Stock Exchange, the fleets, the parties, the wars; long lines of men falling one after the other. The lies. I do not understand them. They hoist their flags, their smiles, their teeth, their tanks, their greed, their calculations, their bellies, and a beauty offers her sex to violence. I see it and I do not believe it. I have my dark and warm little furrow. If I look up, I see a piece of the sky, I can sleep, eat, dream of God, scratch myself. The rest, I do not understand.) (*P.C.*, 288–89)

It is a rhythmic composition based upon well-defined heptasyllabic unities of the fourth verse in each stanza, repeated in most of the longer alexandrine verses that are clearly divided by a caesura at the seventh syllable. The parallel repetition of the fourth verse carries a heavy rhyme formed not only at the end of some verses (vs. 1, 4, 8, 12, 14, and 16), but also in interior positions (vs. 1, 5, 7, 8, 11, 12, 13 twice, 14, 15, and 16). The same rhyme appears seventeen times in this poem of only sixteen verses.

The evident result of this abundance of the same rhyme is a strong sense of repetition, a rhythmic and acoustic insistence very typical of Celaya's versification. The uniformity of the stanzas is also expressive of the same sense of sameness, or routine traditional discursive poetry. The verses that do not conform to the metric pattern (vs. 1 is hendecasyllabic, 2 is thridecasyllabic, 13 and 15 could be considered alexandrine if the caesura is counted as a long pause) are few, and due to their initial position do not affect greatly the general structure of the poem; at most they offer an irregular starting, very much in accordance with the rather inept third verse and cacophonous combination of vocal sounds that make the reader stumble, unable to follow the rhythmic development of the previous verses.

In general, Celaya's poems are extremely monotonous in terms of rhythmic and acoustic patterns; it does not matter if he sometimes uses what looks like free verse, because, in essence, he will still be tuned to a basic rhythmic pattern he will repeat with little flexibility. As a result, occasional irregularities, as in the case of the first stanza in the poem just commented on, appear more as a defect than as an aesthetically pleasing variation of the monotonous metrics. In a sense, this uniformity coincides with sameness of content. The poet has evidently gone too far in his desire to write in simple terms about subjects that everybody talks about in the street, or, still more significant for Celaya's style, in the newspapers. In effect, the reference to the newspaper as a form of knowledge of the true world

has to be related to the contemporary awareness of the mass media
which was to affect postwar literature profoundly.

To contemporary man, reality becomes a very wide and complex
world of worries that tint with dark tones the immediate personal
reality of daily life. Juan de Leceta fights back by hiding, like an
animal, in his "dark and warm little furrow," which insulates him
from a harsh reality he does not want to believe, a reality that he
cannot understand. There, in his own hideout, he can dream of
God, aspire for heavenly beauty, enjoy the sensual life, oblivious
of anything else. This attitude is far from the one that inspired
social poetry; it defines Leceta's existential view of himself, the same
view many Spaniards adopted around the end of the 1940s, when
they turned away from reality and looked for a better world to live
in. But reality was too evident and demanding. Finally, they had
to face it with all of its social inadequacies.

A Turn to Social Awareness

In *Lo demás es silencio,* his first truly social work, published in the
same year as the *Antología consultada,* Celaya strives to dramatize the
situation of a poet like Leceta, or himself. As he says it in the
"Introduction" to a much later edition of the poem, this book is
the most important of all he has written "because in it my personal
problems coincided with a collective problem, typical of a period,
and thus, I was able to deal with the subject in a way both intimate
and social. The period I refer to is that when Lukacs published a
book entitled *Existentialism or Marxism?"*[7] These were the first years
of the 1950s, when the social situation in Spain began to change.
It was the appropriate moment to take seriously the ideas of the
Marxist theorist and rekindle the old revolutionary fire.

Celaya had adopted an increasingly solipsistic, existential attitude
during the literally and politically inactive 1940s. But that same
insistence on the "here" and "now" directed his attention to the
concrete reality of his country. Both forces are represented in the
dramatic poem by a protagonist (the poet) and the Chorus, or the
people and their concrete problems. A third force is represented by
the Messenger, who brings the Good News:

¡A la eh!
Que los trabajadores
se pongan a una en pie.

Caminad todos juntos.
Combatid sin perdones.
Yo anuncio un evangelio
que callaban los dioses.

(A la eh! All workmen stand up at the same time. Walk together. Fight
without giving pardon. I announce a Gospel that the gods have kept
unsaid.) (*P.C.*, 459)

Although the author insists on the personally felt conflict, saying
that both the Protagonist and the Messenger were very much part
of his own self, the poem is too discursive and lacks lyrical expressiveness or dramatic pathos. The extremely long composition dwells
repetitively upon a few basic ideas: the existence of only the material
world, the absurdity of looking for transcendent values and even of
paying too much attention to one's own problems, the utopian
future of a Socialist world in which the great difference will be the
collective consciousness and the collective identity, as summarized
in the last verses of the poem:

No existe un más allá de este dominio.
Existimos nosotros, cotidianos,
y existe bajo un cielo indiferente
el mundo que inventándonos creamos.
Lo demás, inhumano, es un misterio.
Lo demás es vacío.
Lo demás es silencio.
Protagonista
Y en el silencio brillan las estrellas tranquilas
y hay alguien que contempla desde lejos mi vida.

(There is no other world beyond this dominion. We exist, the quotidian
ones, and under an indifferent sky exists the world that we create. The
rest, inhuman, is a mystery. The rest is emptiness. The rest is silence.
Protagonist: And in the silence the quiet stars sparkle. And there is
someone who contemplates my life from afar.) (*P.C.*, 490–91)

The poet is not alone anymore; in contrast to the removed perspective of the individual who reads a newspaper in the safety of his
small refuge, the Chorus stresses the lived experience, the direct
witnessing of human life:

He visto a la muchacha temblorosa de lluvia
y he visto al campesino de fibra retorcida.
He visto al escribiente—¡tan triste aunque él lo ignore!—
y he visto al viejo loco que les habla a los muertos.
He visto en unos ojos de niño qué es el hambre
y he visto en unos ojos de madre qué es el miedo.
He visto la vileza del dolor y el espanto.
He visto y tú me has visto maltratado e indefenso.

(I have seen the girl trembling under the rain, and I have seen the farmer of twisted sinews. I have seen the office clerk—so sad even though he ignores it!—and I have seen the crazy old man who talks to his dead. I have seen in a child's eyes what hunger is, and I have seen what fear is in the mother's eyes. I have seen the vileness of pain and horror. I have seen and you have seen me beaten and defenseless.) (*P.C.*, 489)

This repeated reference to *seeing* is a frequent topic in social poetry: the poet is a witness of what is happening around him. His internal life has been reduced to a minimum because of the powerful vividness of reality. But reality, the concrete presence of it, is absent from the poem, as it is absent from most of Celaya's works. His poetry is too dependent on conceptualizations and rarely touches the concrete. And even when he does touch it, he tends to verbalize in discursive terms something which proves to be, more than an image, a concept of a purely abstract nature. In further interpretations of Celaya's poetry it should be taken into consideration that his essays in prose could demonstrate that his mind works better when abstracting than when thinking in images. Perhaps only then will it be possible to explain the verbose and extremely lengthy poems as a mistake in the medium selected for the communication of a particular message.

Celaya remembers that he failed as a painter in his youth; it will suffice to read some of his poems to understand that it could not have been otherwise; the poet has no visual understanding of reality. His way to relate with the external world is mainly through words, through the abstractions of verbal representations. But even though this characteristic might augur well for the accomplishments of a poet, for Celaya it works in negative ways. The same ability with language that accounts for some verbally effective figures of diction and regular versification in his poems is also responsible for his inability to recognize literary boundaries delimiting effective poetry and mere rhetorical versification.

Lo demás es silencio is a perfect example of Celaya's limitations as a poet. In spite of his intention to write a poem in direct terms and with a clear purpose, Celaya falls into all the rhetorical traps available. The poem is composed mostly in heptasyllabic meter, and the poet is unable to enrich the basic pattern with any rhythmic variation; even when he changes to a different graphic presentation of the text, he continues hammering identical patterns and the reader wonders, why the change in the external form?

The monotonous beat of the mechanically composed verses is further underlined by other unnecessary repetitions. The less disturbing one, although an easy way out for syllable counting, consists in reduplication, which normally should work for emphasis. Not so easy to find, although much more abundant, are groupings by pairs or more elements in coincidence with the verse hemistich. The varieties of this type are too many to analyze, but in essence they give the poem a basic repetitive pattern that (if consciously sought by the poet), make it undoubtedly one of its worst weaknesses. Another troublesome aspect of the poem has to do with the dramatis personae. None of them have a discernible tone or a peculiar voice; they are differentiated mainly for their conceptions, never for their particular identities. This inability to differentiate voices, tones, and attitudes through poetic language is at its worst when the solemn and stilted speech of any of the characters suddenly changes—most of the time for a matter of a few sentences—to a totally different linguistic level. The poet is clearly incapable of judging between an effective variation and plain tastelessness, a problem he had encountered already when writing the Leceta poems.

Dramatic Conflicts

Dramatic structure as a form well suited in dealing with individual conflicts of the poet seemed to be very much liked by Celaya; after trying it in *Lo demás es silencio,* he applied it in other compositions that contain many shortcomings of the first one; these are *Cantata en Aleixandre* [Cantata in Aleixandre, 1959], *El derecho y el revés* [The Right Side and the Wrong Side, 1964], and *Cantata en Cuba,*[8] among others. Taking as models certain political plays from the Republican period, and dramatic techniques from the medieval *autos* as well as elements of expressionism,[9] Celaya simplifies his conflicts and characters to the point of stripping them of all dramatic value. Several of his dramatic poems, though, deal with social conflict, offering a clear-cut opposition between the two forces who fought in the war, and continued fighting, ideologically, during the post-war period.

These poems about a collective subject are as abstract as the ones that deal with the poet's own personal conflicts, because they are inept dramatizations of personal, intellectual, and emotional responses to a rather theoretical world of an ideological nature. *Las resistencias del diamante* [The Resistance of the Diamond, 1957] tries to prove that the four heroic Republicans trying to escape to France become truly heroic and strong in their collective collaboration; they win only as a group. *Vías de agua* [Water Channels, 1960] contrasts the two classes in conflict: the rich and powerful bourgeoisie, and the workers being exploited by them. *Episodios nacionales* [National Episodes, 1962] employs the war as its central theme while attempting to prepare the reader emotionally for the needed faith in the betterment of the world through social ideology.

Cantata en Aleixandre reiterates more or less the same problems represented by the poet, or Protagonist, in *Lo demás es silencio,* except that in this new poem, published at the end of the 1950s, Celaya is no longer so outspokenly Marxist. Another difference is that in this composition he uses verses from Aleixandre, thus pointing to the main conflict present in the older poet, a conflict that took him also in a direction toward socially inspired poetry. The three voices or personae of this dramatic poem are *Las Madres primas* ("The Primigene Mothers"), representing the primary forces of life; *Los Otros* ("The Others"), positivistic men in search of a better world; and *El Poeta* ("The Poet"), who has to fight against the original forces of nature to become one with the rest of men.

For *El derecho y el revés* the description should be very similar, only that the personae in conflict are in this case the *Ingeniero* ("Engineer") and the *Mono* ("Ape"). The latter represents the blindly anguished modern man, while the Engineer is the man who looks for solutions to man's immediate circumstance. Other characters are Ezbá (the feminine figure of passion, from a Basque tradition) and the Zamorros (characters from Basque tradition who in this poem represent the common people). While the Engineer overcomes the doubts of nihilism and helps the Zamorros realize the need to solve their problems, the *Ape* is unable to supersede his original predicament.

Another dramatic composition, the rather short *Cantata en Cuba,* was written during the poet's stay on the island (1967–68). The characters are the *Protagonista* ("Protagonist"), the *Deuteragonista* ("Deuteragonist"), the *Espectadores* ("Audience"), and the *Voz Alta* ("High Voice," or "Loud Speaker"), who recites the texts of Che Guevara. The conflict in this case is limited to two positions within the Communist party, both contraposed by the offstage, magnified voice of the hero, who gives the only appropriate interpretation to the doctrine: to fight the armed revolution. In essence, the dramatic conflict for Celaya takes place in his own mind and does not differ totally from the one posed by the change from the existential Leceta to the Marxist Celaya. It is not at all exceptional, then, that in several cases the discussion centers itself on the subject of poetic language.

Social Poetry versus Aesthetic Poetry

That Celaya tends to see reality as constituted by clear-cut opposing elements is visible in any of his poems from the onset. His long poems are structured precisely as dramatic oppositions; a similar preference for dualism is evident in his shorter compositions. Few indeed are the short poems in which Celaya deals with social topics. Most of them belong to his book *Cantos iberos* [Iberian Songs, 1955], although an occasional composition such as "A Andrés Basterra" [To Andres Basterra], occurs in *Las cartas boca arriba* [Showing One's Cards], wherein the social subject was still absent. This poem, an antecedent to future works, poses the opposition between the workman and the factory owner, only to insist upon their basic identity as men living in a world that seems absurd. The tone of voice is conversational; it has been obtained through the direct address to the workman in words commonly used for oral speech, and through repetitions. There is no real social consciousness in the poem, only the realization that all men suffer because of their common human condition. If the poem has been held up as an example of social poetry it is only because it could be misread to that effect, confusing simple human solidarity with social awareness. In what can be called his social poetry proper, Celaya does not use a conversational tone, but less natural forms of address, as if he had acquired an increased sense of importance.

Cantos iberos are inspired by social commitment. Taking as his main motive the theme of Spain, widely treated by postwar poets, Celaya offers a selection of twenty poems covering his basic set of social ideas. He calls for social change through armed revolution; he points to the class conflict, to the duty for action for future Spain, and mentions the new form of poetry, opposed to the aesthetically centered format of poets not concerned with the present situation. Later on, this generalized political preoccupation with Spain will be directed specifically toward Basque regionalism.

All of the poems in *Cantos iberos* are based upon opposing or contrasting factors, basically between a grim present and a bright future. Out of the twenty compositions, four directly treat the subject of poetry: "La necesidad, la sencillez, la alegría" [Necessity, Simplicity, Happiness], "Hablando en castellano" [Talking in Spanish], "La poesía es un arma cargada de futuro" [Poetry Is a Weapon Loaded with Future], and "Vivir para ver" [Live to See]; several others refer to it. There is no doubt that the speaker, at all moments, is the poet himself, and he is a very special orator, openly addressing other men either by using the apostrophic second person or the first-person plural, which includes himself among others. In the compositions addressed to Spain the apostrophe in second person singular to the motherland is the common method used by most poets. The preaching attitude corresponds to that of a leader, a morally superior individual who directs his fellow men, as is apparent by the abundance of imperatives.

In his categorical way the speaker establishes the opposing aspects of reality:

> Esta fuerza real que llamamos España,
> rabiosa, suficiente,
> no es gótico-galaico-leonesa-romana,
> ni es árabe, ni griega, ni austriaco-castellana.
> Es ibera, terrible, sagradamente arcaica,
> mi materia y mi magia.

(This real force we call Spain, irate, sufficient, is not Gothic-Galaic-Leonese-Roman, neither Arabic, nor Greek, nor Austro-Castillian. It is Iberian, terrible, sacredly archaic, my matter and my magic.) (*P.C.,* 600)

The Francoist exaltation of an Imperial and Catholic Spain is an interpretation of historical facts which Celaya opposes with Spain's

essence and origin: the Iberian. This idea, indicated already in the
title of the book, is stressed several times in other poems of the
collection. "Todo está por inventar" [Everything Has to Be Yet
Invented, *P.C.*, 622–24] not only repeats the ahistorical character
of true Spain, but aims at the future, thus leading to another opposition much repeated in the book—that between present and
future:

> ¡Camaradas!,
> dejémonos de canciones que suenan a más llorar.
> Aquí no ha pasado nada
> y si pasó, no hay que hablar.
> Todo está por inventar.

(Friends!, let us stop singing songs that look like more crying. Nothing
happened here, and if it happened, there is nothing to talk about. Everything has yet to be invented,)

And a little further:

> ¿Quién dijo que España es vieja si aún está por estrenar?
> ¿Qué me importan quince siglos?
> Yo arranco de mis principios iberos y apunto a más.
> Nadie ha dicho todavía lo realmente real.
> ¡Camaradas, a luchar!

(Who said that Spain is old, if yet it has to be inaugurated? Who cares
about fifteen centuries? I start from my Iberian origins and I am pointing
to more. Nobody has said yet the truly real. Friends, let us fight!)

The future idea of Spain is summarized in the terms "liberty"
and "peace," both tacitly opposed to "oppression" and "war," signifying social conflict or fighting among classes. Two literary figures
serve as representations of the lower classes: the Arcipreste de Hita
and Sancho Panza. These aspects are also somewhat related to Blas
de Otero's poetry. In an echo of Otero's *Pido la paz y la palabra,*
Celaya writes: "Sólo quiero respirar / y pido la libertad. / La pido
como mi pueblo porque queremos la paz." ("I only want to breathe,
and I ask for freedom. I ask for it as my people ask for it, because
we want peace," *P.C.,* 619).

The coincidence is almost complete because both writers were committed to a poetic duty: that of claiming rights for their people, being the voice of all men. The reference to classic figures from Spanish literary history is much more effective in Otero's poetry because of the manner in which he combines the technique of allusions and linguistic resonances. While Otero uses a careful critical ear to capture the appropriate common expression, literary citations, and popular sayings in order to create a sense of resonance in his verse, Celaya rarely does so, and seems unaware of the resonances obtainable from well-known terms, names, and expressions.

His poem "A Sancho Panza" [To Sancho Panza, *P.C.,* 606–8] offers his best example of resonance. The name Sancho serves the poet as a good rhythmic and acoustic basis for the creation of several compound names and simple noun-adjective phrases that are used in reduplications and anaphoric repetitions throughout the eighty lines of the poem. They form a basic leitmotiv that sustains the unity of the poem, otherwise somewhat diluted because of Celaya's tendency to use too many lengthy and abstract sentences.

The rhythmical value of the leitmotiv is also based on the number of syllables and positions of the accent, identical to the complete name of Sancho Panza: *Sancho-obrero, Sancho-arcilla, Sancho-pueblo, Sancho-ibero, Sancho-terco* ("Sancho-workman, Sancho-clay, Sancho-people, Sancho-Iberian, Sancho-stubborn"). The exceptions are too few to take into consideration. The basic four syllables and two accents of the pattern account for the rhythm of the complete poem. Four verses (numbers 1, 13, 53, and 77) are dodecasyllabic, formed by three unities of four syllables; they emphasize the metonymic value of the literary character: "Sancho-bueno, Sancho-arcilla, Sancho-pueblo" ("Good Sancho, Sancho-clay, Sancho-people"), "Sancho-vulgo, Sancho-nadie, Sancho-santo" ("Sancho-people, Sancho-nobody, Sancho-Saint"), "Hombre a secas, Sancho-patria, pueblo-pueblo" ("Plainly man, Sancho-fatherland, people-people"), "Sancho-tierra, Sancho-santo, Sancho-pueblo" ("Sancho-earth, Sancho-saint, Sancho-people").

The term *arcilla* represents the same concept as "motherland" and "people"[10] while *nadie* and *santo* are related to Celaya's interpretations of individuality and God in previous books.[11] These four verses occur at the beginning of stanzas and consequently are somewhat easier to scan than if inside a stanza, between the basically octosyllabic meters. Each stanza is formed by four verses, some with eight and some with sixteen syllables; the longer ones have a caesura dividing them into octosyllabic hemistichs.

The assonance is somewhat irregular, but the several cases in which the end of a hemistich rhymes with the end of a verse confirm the impression that the divisions between long and short verses are merely a matter of graphic presentation, with little, if any, effect on the rhythmical aspect of the poem. Celaya tries unsuccessfully to disguise his regular metrics only to satisfy the eye, since in the actual reading the basic pattern becomes fully evident. The language of the poem is a mixture of poetic high language and common expressions; the diction can go from verses as rhetorically tradi- tional—at least in postwar Spain—as "tu valor tan obligado como en la Mancha lo eterno" ("your valor is as much yours as the eternal is of La Mancha") to the too-much-used repetitions and the vulgarity of verses such as "vivimos como vivimos porque tenemos aun tripas" ("We live as we live because we still have guts").

This praising hymn to Sancho-people obviously embodies the opposition between the lower class and the bourgeoisie, represented by the *Señoritos Quijanos* who, in a pun taken from common language, continue living their lies (*viviendo del cuento*). This negative vision of the bourgeois class, to which the poet himself belongs, is repeated throughout his works. Certainly, it constitutes a problem for him as an individual, as is evident in his "A Andrés Basterra," and surely lies at the basis of his conceptions about poetry in Spain.

"Vivir para ver" [Live to See, *P.C.,* 632–37], the last poem of *Cantos Iberos,* is dedicated to "A poet of yesterday," who could easily be himself, although Celaya is thinking in terms of those fascinated with the aesthetic aspects of poetry. Through twenty-two stanzas of eight alexandrine verses each, rhyming irregularly, Celaya dis- cusses the Vanguardist poets he used to like:

> Tal fue la poesía real y delirante
> que ayer me fascinaba, sorbiéndome en sus giros:
> tobogán de caricias verso a verso cursadas
> como una vuelta larga que resbala a ese trozo
> de pueblo palpitante, voraz, real, violento
> que hoy recojo caliente y el mar borra extendiendo.
> Tal fue, nunca mordida, la evidencia increíble
> que se rizaba el rizo con bucles de belleza.

(Such was the real and delirious poetry that yesterday fascinated me and
engulfed me in its whirls: toboggan of caresses that moves from verse to
verse like a long curve that slides past that part of throbbing, hungry,
real, and violent people that I gather warm today, and that the sea erases
by extending it. Such was, never hurt, the evidence that combed itself
with curls of beauty.)

He certainly does not want to pay attention to those merely
beautiful verses:

> Mas no quiero, no quiero ceder a vuestra magia,
> ni al respeto que os debo, ni a ese cómodo elogio
> con que conseguiría la palmada en la espalda.

(But I do not want, I do not want to fall for your beauty, neither to the
respect I owe you, nor yet to that comfortable praise that would gain me
the pat on the back.)

Once again this is a case of conversion from aestheticism to a
human, direct poetry that speaks, as Otero will also say, in Spanish.
One of Celaya's poems is entitled "Hablando en castellano [Talking
in Spanish, *P.C.*, 615–17]. Because the poet has a new audience
and a new duty, to change the present circumstance may produce
a beautiful future:

> Escuchad, camaradas, mis poemas iberos
> de hombre que, recorrido por vuestras mudas vidas,
> quisiera con sus versos lograr, no la belleza,
> sino la acción que pueden y deben los poetas
> promover con sus versos de conmovida urgencia.

(Listen, comrades, to my Iberian poems of a man who, filled by your silent
lives, would like to obtain with his verses not beauty, but the action that
the poets can and must promote with their verses of moving urgency.)

Consequently, the aesthetic poetry of the noncommitted poets
has to be condemned, as he says in his "La poesía es un arma cargada
de futuro" [Poetry Is a Weapon Loaded with Future, *P.C.*, 630–32]:

> Maldigo la poesía concebida como un lujo
> cultural por los neutrales

que, lavándose las manos, se desentienden y evaden.
Maldigo la poesía de quien no toma partido hasta mancharse.

(I condemn the poetry that has been conceived as a luxury by the neutral poets who, washing their hands, do not pay attention, run away. I condemn the poetry of anyone who does not take sides to the point of dirtying himself.)

Conclusion

The powerful force and enthusiasm with which Celaya expressed his Socialist ideas were soon to be overcome by the changing socio-political circumstances in a Spain that was experiencing a fast economic development. During the 1960s the poet began to experiment with other kinds of poetry, although he kept alive and publicly active his "social-poet" persona, by which he had reached notoriety and fame. His fast and changeable pace of production—in poetry as well as in prose—defeats any intention to keep up with it, as well as any desire to follow the poet's evolution, since, after all, he seems to have little new to offer.

A similar problem affects his social books. The few ideas, repeated like slogans, appear to the reader as an ideological plan to be followed rather mechanically, never as a true personal discovery much less as an inspirational force. The fault is not to be found, necessarily, in the poet's personal sense of sincerity, but in his uncontrolled facility to write blindly, as if devoid of the poetic powers of synthesis and emotion. Even when he writes prose, Celaya loses control of his verbal flux, overcoming his readers with words upon words of little effectiveness in matters of communicative value. In his hands, social poetry acquired most of the defects its detractors always cite in order to minimize it as an artistically viable possibility.

Chapter Six
The Dominance of Social Poetry

In the 1950s and early 1960s the literary activity directed toward criticism of the Spanish political and social situations became livelier than ever before. Hoping to be an effective influence in determining the future of their country, writers and intellectuals tried to communicate to the public, and to themselves, a sense of commitment to the immediate circumstances. This attitude was expressed either in open attacks against the inadequacies and injustices of the system or in the critical analysis of its essential aspects.

The Social Preoccupation

In spite of the strong and effective oppressive measures of Franco's regime, or perhaps because of them, Spain's political life during the second and third decades after the Civil War was characterized by a constant tension between the forces of repression and the popular demands for social justice and political freedom. The general mood was tinted by the ideological basis of the fighting. Artists, particularly writers, could not be unaware of the situation, and many of them felt the need to take an active part in the battle. The sociopolitical aspect of man's condition became a fixation with a people who could not forget a recent violent conflict which was not yet finished, as the international cold war constantly recalled.

The theories of commitment in the arts and the writing of social literature were to become characteristic of this period. Significantly, the figure and works of Antonio Machado, who had died in France immediately following a strenuous escape from the triumphant Nationalist army at the end of the war, were respectfully admired, mainly because of Machado's involvement as a man and poet in the political fighting during the troubled years of the Republic.[1] Likewise, the works of Miguel Hernández, a poet who had suffered the fatal consequences of his political commitment, were exalted as another example of the power of poetry against the forces of oppression.[2]

Numerous poems and books of poetry with a social content were published during the period. Editors and critics were instrumental in causing the increasing literary fascination with the social themes and topics among the public and the poets themselves.[3] Periodical publications, literary prizes, and editorial houses encouraged the production and consumption of such literature; consequently, the number of authors who declared themselves socially committed poets grew in proportion with the market and its demands for a literature offering an alternative to the official propaganda.

In his anthology of social poetry, published in 1965, Leopoldo de Luis—himself a social poet—offered a selection of some thirty authors, which he considered reason enough to support the claim that social poetry was a strong and evident manifestation of the contemporary interest among philosophers, artists, and all men in the "common human destiny."[4] Although partially correct in his judgment, close reading of the selected poems convinces any careful reader of the extremely loose critical standards of the anthologist— few of the poets he included in the anthology have a poetic work that can be considered more than a mere, fashionable formula.

Two Poetic Promotions

Among those poets who, included in de Luis's anthology, deserve the attention of the literary historian because of the quality of their works it is possible to distinguish two main age groups or promotions. The first one is formed by those born between 1902 and 1918, who consequently developed intellectually before the Civil War. These include Angela Figuera Aymerich (1902), Victoriano Crémer (1906), Gabriel Celaya (1911), Blas de Otero (1916–79), and Gloria Fuertes (1918).

The second group embraces those poets born not less than twelve years before the Civil War, and who thus were too young to have an intellectually mature memory of the prewar years. Their literary formation takes place mainly in the years immediately following the end of the war. They include Angel González (1925), José Agustín Goytisolo (1928), José Angel Valente (1929), and Jaime Gil de Biedma (1929). To these should be added at least the name of José

Manual Caballero Bonald (1926), who was not included in the anthology and perhaps others.

The members of both groups, excepting Celaya, published all their works after 1945. But since social poetry was as much a cause as a consequence of the new sensibility developed in the 1950s, social poets wrote their most committed works only after 1952; by then, writers, critics, and the public were ready to give full attention to the social theme in literature and the arts, in spite of the strict controls of governmental censorship.

Thus, Otero and Celaya, as already seen, managed to voice their ideologically based criticism in a poetry that had many of the traits of programmatic and propagandistic literature. Other poets, less distinctly faithful to a given political ideology, tried to follow their example; while still other, younger ones sought improvement of their literary accomplishments, focusing their attention on the aesthetic quality of the poem as well as on its thematic validity. These younger authors brought with them a more complex understanding of the poet's position in contemporary society, and even their views on society itself were less categorical than those of the older group.

Although the members of both "promotions" or groups were simultaneously writing social poetry, there are fundamental differences between the two trends, particularly in their conceptions of the essence of poetry. While the older poets failed to create, as a group, an aesthetically mature poetry, the younger writers, having a keener sense of artistic responsibility, and being less limited by a shortsighted social view on literature, developed an artistically demanding language that set the basis for significant development of the lyric genre in the Spain of the 1970s.

A Shortlived Poetic Fashion

With few exceptions, none of the poets who best represent Spanish social commitment produced an extensive and continuous work. Although most of the younger ones continued writing well into the 1970s, only José Angel Valente and Angel González have maintained a regular, albeit slow, rhythm of publication. With the poets of the first promotion the situation is a little different, only because several of them have stopped publishing new works. In summary, the preeminence of social poetry can be limited to a period of roughly ten years, ending in the mid-1960s or a little later.

These limits are certainly discernible in Otero's and Celaya's literary production. Both evolved in their poetic careers from a merely personal interest in man's destiny to a doctrinal defense of social justice in an immediate and concrete world. When the cherished new society failed to materialize, and the socioeconomic forces in Spain seemed to belie their utopian hopes, they reacted in rather similar ways: Celaya abandoned social verse almost completely, moving toward what he considered a more up-to-date poetic fashion; Otero reduced still more his already slow pace in writing and publishing new works.

Other poets of their age group reacted comparably. Victoriano Crémer, who had begun his active poetic life only after the Civil War, did not last long in the interest of the public or the critics; his *Poesía total (1944–1966)* [All the Poetry (1944–1966)], published in 1967, may be regarded as the final editorial recognition of his historical value as a poet of a period already gone. Angela Figuera Aymerich, whose last book, *Toco la tierra* [I Touch the Earth], was published in 1962, did not even see her few complete works published in a well-known collection until much later, when, in 1973, a younger editor prepared, with an almost archaeological perspective, her *Antología total (1948–1969)* [Complete Anthology (1948–1969)].

The silence of these poets before the Civil War and again, following a few years of literary productivity, is revelatory of the very specific and limited objective of their work and of its total dependency on socio-political circumstances, including literary fashion. Particularly representative of this situation are the cases of two women writers whose works were considered, for a while, to be excellent poetry, and today are considered as little more than examples of the period's questionable literary taste.

Angela Figuera Aymerich

Born in 1902, Angela Figuera did not begin to publish her poetry until 1948. Of the utmost interest in her work is the assumption of her condition of woman and mother in a country that had been torn apart by a fratricidal war. Her first book, *Mujer de barro* [Clay Woman, 1948], collects brief poems about feminine love for man and son. She prefers direct, simple language, with very concrete images that express bluntly her profound sense of being; "Tierra" [Earth] is a poem that prefigures the title of her last book:

> Tendida, vientre a vientre con la tierra
> —humedecida y blanda;
> abierta a la semilla, a los viriles
> rayos del sol—, pegué mi boca cálida
> a sus mullidas sienes: "Yo también,
> yo también paro, hermana.
>
> Tú y yo, cauce profundo de la vida.
> Tierra las dos . . . ¡Hermana, hermana, hermana
> . . . !"

(I lie down, my womb against the womb of the earth—the humid and soft earth; open to the seed, to the virile rays of the sun—and put my warm lips against her soft temple: "I also give birth, sister. You and I, we are the profound river bed of life. We are both earth . . . Sister, sister, sister . . . !")[5]

Her voice becomes more dramatic and forceful in *Vencida por el ángel* [Defeated by the Angel, 1950], *El grito inútil* [The Useless Scream, 1952], *Víspera de la vida* [The Day Before Life, 1953), and *Los días duros* [The Hard Days, 1953], which deal with subjects related to the war and postwar circumstances. "Egoísmo" [Selfishness, *A.T.*, 43–44] opposes the "inside," where the individual keeps himself safe from the external world, and the "outside," or that same world of harrowing realities. The composition follows a structure common to many of Figuera's poems. She builds up a melodramatic view of reality through anaphoric stanzas, or verses, that accumulate "tremendist" images to the point of loathing. The figure of the woman and mother is rarely absent in these overdone enumerations:

> Fuera, las madres dóciles que alumbran
> con terrible alarido;
> las que acarrean hijos como fardos
> y las que ven secarse ante sus ojos
> la carne que parieron y renuevan
> su grito primitivo.
>
> Fuera, los niños pálidos, creados
> al latigazo rojo del instinto,
> y que la vida, bruta, dejó solos

como una mala perra su camada,
y abren los anchos ojos asombrados
sobre las rutas áridas,
mordiendo con sus bocas sin dulzura
los largos días duros

(Outside, the docile mothers that give birth with terrible scream; the ones who carry their sons like bales, and the ones who see helplessly the flesh they engendered dry away and renew their primitive cry. Outside, the pale children, created under the red blow of instinct; the children whom life, a brute, left alone, like a bad bitch abandons her cubs; and they open their wide astonished eyes at the arid roads while biting with their unsweetened mouths the long and harsh days.)

The desperation and anguish caused by poverty, war, and its consequences are also expressed through her view on womanhood:

¿Qué vale una mujer? ¿Para qué sirve
una mujer viviendo en puro grito?
¿Qué puede una mujer en la riada
donde naufragan tantos superhombres
y van desmoronándose las frentes
alzadas como diques orgullosos
cuando las aguas discurrían lentas?

(What is a woman worth? What use is a woman who lives in one cry? What can a woman do in the flood where so many supermen drown and the high foreheads, built up like proud dams when the waters ran slow, begin to collapse? *A.T.*, 51.)

A similar feeling of ineptitude and impotence is ascribed to the poet, who must sing and write in a world of violence and injustice; the poet is a different type of person who suffers much more than the rest of men. This enlarged idea of the poet explains, to a certain extent, the conception of poetry as a form of communication, and also a viable way to produce changes in man and society. It also explains why poets like Celaya and Figuera tend to exaggerate their emotions and look for solemnity and grandiloquence even when claiming the need for a direct and common language.

In her composition "Poeta" [Poet, *A.T.*, 80–81] Angela Figuera begins in rather simple language: "Más de un día me duele ser poeta. Me duele / tener labios, garganta, que se ordenan al canto. / Es tan fácil vivir cuando sólo se vive / mudo y simple, esquivando la pesquisa y el vértigo." ("More than once it hurts to be a poet. It hurts to have lips and thoughts that are directed to sing. It is so easy to live when you simply exist, mute and uncomplicated, avoiding the questioning and the fear of emptiness"). Her conviction as to the superiority of the poet over the simple man—a rather contradictory conception for one who conceives of herself as a social poet—leads to an almost cosmic description in terms recalling a long-forgotten style and attitude: "Océanos, ciclones, bosques, astros habitan / en el ámbito estrecho que su cráneo circunda. / Olas, aves, raíces, pulsaciones, acordes, / por la red de los nervios se le enroscan vibrando." ("Oceans, cyclones, forests, stars live in the narrow space circumscribed by his skull. Waves, birds, roots, pulses, tunes twist around his net of nerves vibrating").

Carried away by her desire to communicate a sense of outrage, and the consequent critical attitude of the speaker, Angela Figuera exaggerates her techniques, evincing her lack of literary maturity. Her style is melodramatic; the extensive sentences are grouped in irregular stanzas of regular unrhymed verses following different patterns of repetitiveness. The voice of the tense speaker cries constantly at its highest pitch, while the subjects are mostly negative and sad.

She offers, though, a few solutions or plans for action, none of which is social in character. The idea that women should rebel against the violent masculine world, and stop procreating, is certainly radical in principle:

> Serán las madres todas rehusando
> ceder su vientre al trabajo inútil
> de concebir tan sólo hacia la fosa.
> De dar fruto a la vida cuando saben
> que no ha de madurar entre sus ramas.
> No más parir abeles y caínes.

(It will be all the mothers who refuse to devote their wombs to the useless task of conceiving only for the tomb. Of giving fruit to life when they know that it will not ripen on the branches. No more giving birth to the Abels and Cains.) (A.T., 55–56)

In a more constructive mood, she encourages women to speak for their offspring—"Madres del mundo, tristes paridoras, / gemid, clamad, aullad por vuestros frutos." ("Mothers of the world, sad givers of life: cry, call out, and scream for your fruit," *A.T.*, 80). Even more, they should fight against masculine violent ways:

> A la embestida seca de los machos
> que olvidan la pulida reverencia,
> la rosa, el madrigal y aquellos besos
> en el extremo de la mano esquiva,
> hay que oponer lo recio femenino.
> El sexo puro, leal, íntegro, casto
> a fuerza de arrancar viejas guirnaldas
> de trapo con olor a hipocresía.
>
> Ya no podemos acunar la débil
> carne del hijo en un regazo tibio
> de raso y plumas: hay que sostenerla
> con fuertes manos, apoyarla adrede
> en el inquieto suelo, preparando
> con firme decisión su andar futuro.

(Against the dry attack of the male who forgets the polite reverence, the rose, the madrigal, and those kisses at the tip of the timid hand, we must oppose feminine strength. Pure sex, loyal, honest sex, chaste by its constant pulling out of the old garlands made of rags smelling of hypocrisy. We cannot now cradle the weak flesh of the child in a warm embrace of satin and feathers: we have to grab it with strong hands, and stand it on purpose on the restive floor, thus preparing it, with firm decision, for its future walking.) (*A.T.*, 78)

As for her vision of the poet, Figuera also shows vacillation; at one point she sees the poet as totally useless, and at others she conceives him as a necessary voice in a troubled world. In "Silencio" [Silence, *A.T.*, 57] she declares that "Ser poeta es superfluo." ("To be a poet is superfluous") and that "Ser poeta es inútil en un mundo acosado" ("To be a poet in a troubled world is useless"). One of the last verses of the poem—"Mejor fuera callarse. Licenciar la metáfora" ("It would be better to keep quiet, to discharge the metaphor")— reappears in another poem, "Epílogo a Blas de Otero" [Epilogue for Blas de Otero, *A.T.*, 62–63].

> Y yo llegué a decirte: *Mejor fuera el silencio.*
> *Mejor fuera callarse. Licenciar la metáfora.*

Y ver si a duras penas o a duras alegrías
abrimos un camino al cabo de la calle.

(And I even told you: It would be better to be silent. It would be better
to keep quiet. To discharge the metaphor. And see if with pains or
happiness we could open a road at the end of the street.)

The same Blas de Otero—from whose work she appropriates (in
this example) the technique of playing with common expressions,
and the references to "silence" and the "dead-end street"—also
provides her formula for poetic action:

Pido la paz y la palabra. Pido
un aire sosegado, un cielo dulce,
un mar alegre, un mapa sin fronteras,
una argamasa de sudor caliente
sobre las cicatrices y fisuras.

(I ask for peace and the right to speak. I ask for a calm air, a sweet sky,
a happy sea, a map without frontiers, a mortar of warm sweat over the
wounds and cracks.) (*A.T.*, 100)

The speaker in this poem, as indicated by its title, is the *Hombre
naciente* ("Man being born"), a new generation, the sons—to whom
Figuera addresses several poems—of those who fought the war; he
is the new man who brings hope for the future:

Pido la paz y pido a mis hermanos
los hijos de mujer por todo el mundo
que escuchen esta voz y se apresuren.
. . . .
Después, que vengan a nacer conmigo.
Haremos entre todos cuenta nueva.
Quiero vivir. Lo exijo por derecho.
Pido la paz y entrego la esperanza.

(I ask for peace, and I ask my brothers, the sons of women all over the
world, to listen to this voice and to hurry. . . . Then, let them come
to be born with me. Between all of us we will begin from scratch. I want
to live. I demand it as my right. I ask for peace and I deliver hope.) (*A.T.*,
100)

Language, stylistic techniques, subject matter, and tone are all extremely simplified in Figuera's works. A sense of a raw, exaggerated, and self-indulgent pain appears so strongly stressed in verse after verse, and poem after poem, that only a few minutes of reading suffice to counteract any form of empathy with the speaker; the roughly structured poems appear naked in all their rhetorical assemblage, and the aesthetic experience ends in displeasure.

Gloria Fuertes

Still more inclined toward directness and overdramatization is Gloria Fuertes, perhaps the one writer who managed among the social poets to achieve the much-desired communication through poetry. She deserves to be studied among other social poets precisely because she was able to create a popular audience for her work, much like Manuel Gerena, the poet and singer, has done.[6] Both appeal to the common people; Gerena does it via the highly impressive *cante jondo* of deep popular roots; Fuertes, by means of a poetry well-suited for recitation in public. In effect, Gloria Fuertes's poetry is markedly oral;[7] in a sense, it is the transcription of an improviser who lets herself be inspired by the rhythm and sound of the voice when addressing a crowd.

Another aspect that renders her poetry easily accessible to an emotionally ready audience is the directness of her speech, direct in two senses: in its sincere tone of openness and bluntness and in the simple, straightforward language of common everyday use, with brief and often-repeated sentences, slang expressions, and innuendoes. She has developed an easily identifiable poetic persona, whose defiant and boorish language reveals a radically rebellious attitude. Her rebellion, though, has been mistaken for social commitment; it is, rather, the more generalized unsubmissiveness of a strong, individualistic character who feels restrained in any social order: "Yo la rebelde a todos los feudales" ("I, the rebel against all the feudal lords").[8]

With absolute disregard for anything structured, her poems, her books, and her own views on reality as seen through her works are shapeless and unstructured. All seem to originate spontaneously as an immediate response to stimuli: the speaker bursts into words, stopping only when the flow of closely related sounds cannot prolong itself further. The easy play with sounds and its many available interactions are quite evident at the end of "A X" (To X).

> Te amo,
>   porque eres mi amo
>   —mi amor y mi amo—
>   y si quiero mi siervo,
>   pero no quiero.

(I love you because you are my lord—my love and lord—and if I want, you are my servant, but I do not want it.) (*A.P.*, 193)

The titles of her different books give an idea of Fuertes's evolution from a purely sentimental self-compassion in *Isla ignorada* [Unknown Island, 1950] to the fashionable subject of the social outcast in *Antología y Poemas del suburbio* [Anthology and Poems of the Slum, 1954], together with other topics of social criticism in *Aconsejo beber hilo* [I Advise Drinking Thread, 1954]. The rest of her work includes *Ni tiro, ni veneno, ni navaja* [Neither a Shot, not Poison, nor Knife. 1966], *Poeta de guardia* [Poet on Guard, 1968], *Cómo atar los bigotes del tigre* [How to Tie the Tiger's Whiskers, 1969], and some children's books.

A certain penchant for the humorous in her verses also appears in the titles of her books, as well as in her use of allusive techniques similar to the ones used by Otero. But in Fuertes's style the resonance functions with less subtlety than in the older poet thus, when she takes as a model for one of her poems a Catholic prayer, as Otero does, she cannot avoid overstressing the procedure. Only a few verses of "Oración" [Prayer, *A.P.*, 81] will suffice to demonstrate:

> Padre nuestro que estás en la tierra,
> en el surco,
> en el huerto,
> en la mina,
> en el puerto,
> en el cine,
> en el vino,
> en la casa del médico.
> Padre nuestro que estás en la tierra,
> donde tienes tu gloria y tu infierno
> y tu limbo que está en los cafés
> donde los burgueses beben su refresco.

(Our father who art in earth, in the furrow, in the orchard, in the mine, in the seaport, in the movie house, in the wine, in the doctor's house. Our father who art in earth, where you have your glory and your hell, and your limbo in the coffee houses where the bourgeoisie drink their refreshments.)

The humorous reference to the vacuous middle class does not fit in with the otherwise serious, although overdone, transformation of the prayer's words. It could also be that Fuertes was not planning on a play of words when comparing a coffeehouse with limbo; but that would not be her style. Playing with words and common expressions is precisely her most-used skill, so much so that she almost always carries it too far:

> He estado al borde de la tuberculosis
> al borde de la cárcel,
> al borde de la amistad,
> al borde del arte,
> al borde del suicidio,
> al borde de la misericordia,
> al borde de la envidia,
> al borde de la fama,
> al borde del amor,
> al borde de la playa,
> y poco a poco me fue dando sueño
> y aquí estoy durmiendo al borde
> al borde de despertar.

(I have been on the verge of getting tuberculosis, on the verge of going into jail, on the verge of friendship, on the verge of art, on the verge of committing suicide, on the verge of mercy, on the verge of envy, on the verge of fame, on the verge of love, on the verge of the beach, and little by little I was becoming sleepy, and here I am, sleeping at the edge, on the verge of waking up.) (*A.P.*, 77)

For Gloria Fuertes the principle of communication applies for poetry above all and beyond any other value. Her straightforwardness of expression denounces not only a desire to be understood by all, but also reveals a lack of poetic inventiveness and acumen. If Celaya makes of his social verse an extremely discursive medium, Fuertes, in turn, deprives hers of all intellectual aspects, making of it an empty din of rhythmic monotony, easy puns, and phonetic echoes in repetitions, rhymes, and wordplay. Her poetry carries to an extreme the use of common language and of resonance, as proposed by Otero, minimizing the topical aspects of the social theme.

The Younger Poets

The younger social poets, who because of their age began to publish their first books about 1955, contrast notably with the older ones, particularly with those who made exaggerated use of rhetorical methods in order to make their voices better understood by a supposedly popular and uncultured public. Working independently of each other at the beginning, a few of the young poets coincided in some essential aspects of style, attitude, and poetic objectives and later developed certain intellectual friendships and collaborations.

One might speak of a group when referring to them—although they never formally established an organization with common literary objectives and planned literary policies—not only because they belong to the same age group, but also because in their general attitudes and points of view with respect to their world, and of poetry, they were manifestly similar, despite their individual differences. Other poets of their age who could be seen as belonging to the same chronological or generational group do not reach a comparable level of poetic commitment, and thus should be considered as only partially related to the very few who made valuable contributions to social poetry.

Taking these facts into consideration, it becomes clear that the classification of those younger poets under generational denominations such as "generation of Rodríquez-Brines," "generation of 1950," or "of half century," or "second postwar generation" is not accurate enough for the historian of social poetry in postwar Spain. A better description might be obtained from the labels "generation of social realism," or "of critical realism," even though the generational character does not apply at all, since only some of these young poets are to be considered as belonging to such literary schools.[9]

In other words, the young poets commencing their literary careers around 1955 did not necessarily approve or follow the social trend just initiated by their elders; on the other hand, not all of those who did espouse the socially directed poetry brought to their works a new light on the matter or an improved literary language. Only the very few poets who were able to do otherwise, and to transcend the immediacy of a poetic trend, deserve individualized inclusion in a study of social poetry. The rest are valuable mostly in terms of statistics to support the observation that social poetry was very much cultivated in the said period.

Social Realism

José María Castellet's *Viente años de poesía española* [Twenty Years of Spanish Poetry], published in 1960, is a fundamental document for the history of Spanish letters during the period between 1939 and 1959.[10] In the introductory study to this anthology of postwar Spanish poets, Castellet supports the theory that lyric poetry in Spain has evolved from decadent symbolism to a new, active and strong social realism, represented by the younger poets maturing in the postwar years. In essence he is applying to contemporary poetry the same interpretation other writers were using in reference to the novel, the theater, and the arts.

This understanding of the cultural process of their country is the result of a sociological and critical perspective that corresponds, roughly, to some of the poet's own ideological points of view. It must be remembered that Castellet himself belongs—because of his age and his friendship with some of its members—to a group formed by several influential young intellectuals and poets centered in Barcelona who supported similar positions. Social realism, however, was also being discussed in Madrid in these same years.

As early as 1952, the dramatist Alfonso Sastre had published in *Indice de Artes y Letras,* a Madrid periodical, an article titled "¿Qué es el social-realismo?"[11] The ideas expressed there, as well as in his book *Drama y sociedad* [Drama and Society, 1956] and in his article-manifesto "Arte como construcción" (*Acento Cultural,* 1958), are summarized in the first article of his *Anatomía del Realismo* (1965). Discussing all forms of literature and art, he points to several fundamental aspects of social realism visible in the young poets who published their first books after 1950.

Social realism is not a literary formula, says Sastre, but a conscious acceptance of the urgent need for an art adequate to the present, to a time in which "the social has become the supreme category of human preoccupation."[12] This is what he calls, in words also used by Celaya, an "urgent art." He adds also that the social-realist writer "considers that his work has repercussions in the social body and is able, then, to contribute to its degeneration, or its purifying revolution" (*A.R.*, 21). In other words, the writer's intentions transcend the artistic effects of his work.

But at no moment does Sastre say that this preference for social effectiveness implies an abandonment of the aesthetic values of the literary work. On the contrary, and opposing the antiaesthetic attitudes of poets like Celaya and Fuertes, this critic insists on the need for an aesthetically pleasing work: "Only an art of great aesthetic quality is able to transform the world. We call attention to the radical uselessness of the artistic work that is not well done. That work appears to us many times in the shape of what we could call a pamphletary art. This art is unacceptable from the artistic point of view (because of its aesthetic degeneration), and from the social point of view (because of its lack of usefulness)" (*A.R.*, 18). The optimum social-realist literature, then, produces an "aesthetic emotion" which has an ethical core that remains with the reader after the aesthetic effect has dissipated. This ethical factor is the essential "political projection" of social art. Artists and writers are themselves highly ethical individuals who cannot be coerced externally; they are fully responsible for their moral and artistic conduct because they know that art, "for the simple fact that reveals the structure of reality, accomplishes . . . an act of justice" (*A.R.*, 17).

Basic to Sastre's theory is the idea that art is precisely "a revealing representation of reality" (*A.R.*, 16). The poet's duty consists mainly in making possible such revelation, a revelation that could be accomplished by different techniques and could refer to any of the many "provinces of being" (*A.R.*, 17). Reality, in turn, is nothing but a process of realizations of revelations throughout man's history. It seems obvious, then, to suppose that poets will also be experiencing this process and thus conceive of themselves as historically and socially determined. Quite understandably some younger poets, who did not always write an openly direct social poetry, can be included among the more evident social poets. They had a conception of themselves as individuals, and of the world as exterior reality or circumstances that are properly social. They see themselves as historically concrete men living in a concrete time and space—here and now—which cannot be denied or ignored. Besides, they dutifully assume this temporal condition and try to translate it into a new kind of socially committed poetry.

Colliure

Castellet relates this historically determined poetry of the new social poets with Antonio Machado's theoretical principles about the lyric genre, which in the height of social realism was briefly and significantly reduced to a definition of poetry as *palabra en el tiempo* ("word in time"): "The poets of the new generation tend, in general, toward a realist poetry that, in a wide sense, takes as its own the postulates advocated by Antonio Machado."[13] In effect, the abundance of poems about Machado, or dedicated to him; the numerous citations and epigraphs taken from the works of the master from the Generation of '98; the comments about his poetry and theories are all indisputable indications of his strong influence upon the way the postwar groupings saw poetry and the poet's duty. Quite expressive of this approval and admiration for Machado's teachings is the fact that for the twentieth anniversary of his death a large group of poets and writers crossed the frontier into France to pay tribute to the poet at his tomb, in the town of Colliure, where he had died in 1939 after fleeing from the triumphant Nationalist army. This anniversary and the ceremonial homage to the Republican poet mark, undoubtedly, the highest point in the history of postwar social poetry in Spain.

"Colliure," the poetry collection created in 1961 and directed by Castellet, tried to maintain a continuity in the publication of social verse as inspired in Machado's example. By 1965, when the collection was discontinued, it had published only a few titles, and not all of them could be considered as characteristically social in inspiration.[14] In a generalization that should have excluded more than one name of the poets published by "Colliure," J. Lechner remarks that the volumes of the collection coincide in the same type of language, "somber and with a tendency to prosaism."[15]

This observation applies particularly but not exclusively to the younger poets and corresponds to what Castellet had cited as influences of Machado's style in works of the new realist poets: "with respect to the form, they are inclined toward a simplicity of expression, toward the colloquial language found in the best poems by Machado."[16] The so-called "simplicity" certainly does not mean directness of communication through everyday, common language, but quite the contrary; it is the result of a search for new, more profound meaning in man's condition, which cannot exclude the historical and social circumstances.

As does Sastre, Castellet underlines the historical conditioning of man, and its extreme importance in the works of the new poets: "The theme of those poets is the historic man who belongs in a world in transformation, and who, knowingly or not, is dramatically urged by the circumstances that make him commit himself to his time" (*C.S.P.E.*, 110). For the Spanish poets these circumstances are postwar Spain and its immediate antecedent, the Civil War: "In all of them throbs the need to penetrate, to understand, and even to assume the meaning of a civil war" (*C.S.P.E.*, 111). The most valuable aspect of writing, for them, is not the communication of established conceptions or the propagandizing of a particular ideological outlook of the world. What they want, above all, is to inquire about the reality of their personal, historical circumstance, which has been purposely veiled and obscured by ignorance and deceit.

Truth and lie—light and darkness—become one of the most important literal and symbolic aspects of language; at the basis of it is the need for knowledge and understanding of the historical condition. Their method of inquiry—poetry—presupposes a careful consideration of their medium—poetic language—and of its possibilities as a tool suited for their purposes. It also entails questioning the essence of Spain, their fatherland, and reviewing their memories about the experience of growing up in that land at such a difficult time. The following chapter will discuss these matters as seen in the works of the best representative young social-realist poets.

Chapter Seven
Poetry as a Form of Knowledge

Although equally as committed to bettering Spain's political and social circumstances as de Nora, Otero, and Celaya, some of the younger poets who began their literary careers around the mid-1950s produced a type of poetry radically different from that written by their immediate predecessors and by most of their contemporaries. In effect, if most of the new poets saw themselves as followers of their elders' ideals of poetic *engagement,* a few among them reacted strenuously against the aesthetically simplified idea of poetry as merely a form of communication, progressing toward the development of a theory of poetic language and its relationship to society. They were to become in the ensuing years the harbingers of the new directions taken by Spanish literary thought.

The first voices of a socially inspired poetry had reacted to the post–Civil War political situation in either a blindly emotional protest or in almost equally blind ideological propaganda, thus setting the tone of pathos characteristic of social verse. The newer poets, in a lesser or greater degree, opted for a more objective critical attitude and were able to improve the aesthetic quality of the social poem; but only the very few able to transcend the limited frame of poetic philistinism could achieve the expressive freedom of an authentic language. Their triumph over the deadening formulaic limitations and stereotyped style of social protest meant the disappearance of the obviously direct poetic discourse, in favor of a much subtler understanding of linguistic communicativeness.

Poetic Autodidacticism

The younger poets matured intellectually during the first postwar years, attending the dogmatically controlled schools of the triumphant conservative faction of Catholic Spain. Their schooling, then, was marked by a frequent lack of veritable masters and the narrow-minded misinformation of Fascist propaganda. Autodidacticism was the alternative available to those who could not accept or dispute the official teachings. Extremely critical, and despondent concerning values, the information and methods proposed by their teachers and by postwar society generally, they had necessarily to engage in an independent search for meaning and truth.

This hopeful search took them to what lay beyond their limited world—the rest of Europe and also prewar Spain. Their lack of conformity with Froncoist Spain manifested itself in strong, personal ethical values, intellectual acuteness, and a sense of uniqueness. Having pursued university studies and belonging largely to the bourgeoisie, they could consider themselves members of an elite with important responsibilities toward the country. It is this ethical sense of social duty which most essentially makes them social poets, although they avoided the easy formulas of the earlier poetry, conceived as a message to be understood by the majority of men. Their own compositions had to be more complex, both in subject and form.

The familiarity these poets had with European and prewar Spanish literature accounts for their more refined conceptions of the poem and its social effectiveness. What they did not like about other social poetry then being written in Spain was the primacy it gave to communicativeness, because by so doing it deprived itself of poetry's essential quality—lyric intention and insight. They could not approve a poetic language conceived only as a direct transmission of fixed ideas and predetermined points of view. Poetry, for them, becomes more than a loaded linguistic message: it is a particular form of verbal expression differing from other forms of speech in its aesthetic and gnostic values.

Poetry as Knowledge

In the introduction to the *Antología de "Adonais"* ["Adonais" Anthology, 1953], Vincente Aleixandre commented that the distinctive character of the new poetry represented therein was "its desire to communicate and to reach the largest possible number of people."[1] These words seemed to come as a confirmation of his idea that poetry is a form of human communication. But at the same time that the masterly voice of Aleixandre was acclaiming the new poets for their directness of expression and for their preoccupation with the common man, Carlos Barral, a young writer from Barcelona, refuted the interpretation of poetry as mainly a form of communication among men. In his article "Poesía no es comunicación" [Poetry Is Not Communication],[2] he exposed contrary ideas that would be accepted by poets of his same age group as more appropriate descriptions of poetry. According to Barral, post–Civil War poetry was largely boring and constituted a regression in poetic development. Religious poetry, the poetry of everyday life, and the poetry of social concerns appear to him as very similar, and quite unconvincing as an art form. They are the consequence of a "series of theoretical ghosts: the message, the communication, the accessibility to the majority of men." All of these, he continues, are "subjects of our times that coerce the creative impulse" of the writer. The essence of poetry lies in the poetic process itself, in what Barral calls the "poetic fact" or the autonomous moment of creativity. Both the writer and the reader participate, in different ways, in this creative act that defines poetry.

Barral is expounding, in other words, a theory of poetic knowledge or experience totally ignored or excluded by the theory of communication as interpreted by the social poets. In their view the writing of poetry "implies the existence of a psychological content that could be explained linguistically even before the poem's composition." Barral's theory, on the contrary, postulates that the psychological instance prior to the poem's composition exists in the poet's mind as an indefinite conception and comes to light only by means of the poetic process: "The poet ignores the lyrical content of his poem until the poem itself exists."

The same idea is later elaborated by another young Catalan poet from Barcelona, Jaime Gil de Biedma. Addressing himself to the subject in an article entitled "Poesía y comunicación" [Poetry and Communication],[3] he declares: "There is another way to interpret the term communication, and it is much subtler [than the one proposed by the social poets]: it is based on an explicit recognition of the autonomy of the creative act. The possible poem appears, at the beginning, as an indefinite spiritual state that has an affective sign, and it becomes more specific along the creative process: the vicissitudes of this one give to it a form and a content." This amounts to saying that the poet comes to know reality, or better yet, communicates to himself an understanding of reality, precisely via the poetic process.

Both Barral and Gil de Biedma underline the "revealing" character of poetry as opposed to a mere transmission of a given content, stressing the power or capacity of poetic language as an instrument to inquire deeply into the mysteries of reality. This view of poetry, akin to prewar conceptions of a surrealistic nature, is cited in 1959 by one critic as an important new development in postwar Spanish poetry: "The poets of today return poetry to its original destiny; they hope to live it, and to use it as an instrument of knowledge."[4] It is typical of the period to insist upon art's functionalism, of which poet and critics alike were totally convinced.

By 1962 Aleixandre himself acknowledged these new views on poetry and their aesthetic consequences. In the prologue to a new, amplified *Segunda antología de "Adonais"* [Second "Adonais" Anthology], he affirms in reference to the poets who had become known in the 1950s: "If a few years ago what mattered was, above all, the clarification of the language, today—once the battle has been won by the former ones [the older poets]—the new poets coincide in the unavoidable conquest, even though some of them still maintain the exemplary sense of urgency for communication and others try to make poetry more translucent by means of a careful art in a new, significant writing."[5]

With his careful wording Aleixandre tried to avoid creating the impression that there existed a profound disagreement between the different groups of poets writing at the end of the 1950s. Critics have insisted also on the apparent harmony among those who supported the view of poetry as a form of direct communication with the people and the ones who preferred a more complex interpretation of their poetic activity.[6] But Barral's and Gil de Biedma's articles indicate that an important sector of the younger group did not follow or approve the example of the older social poets, and the newcomers with new conceptions set the basis for renewal of lyrical language in the rapidly changing Spain of the 1960s.

A Revealing Anthology

As was pointed out in the previous chapter, during the 1950s and 1960s there coincided in Spain two types of social poets, whose main difference was their opposing preferences for either understanding poetry as simplified communication or as an instrument of knowledge whose function resembled revelation. *Poesía última* [Latest Poetry, 1963], an anthology prepared by Francisco Ribes—the same one who ten years before had been responsible for the *Antología consultada*—exemplifies this situation and constitutes a good document for the study of trends in Spanish poetry of the period.

In this new anthology Ribes limits the number of poets included to only five; of these, Eladio Cabañero, Angel González, and Carlos Sahagún declare themselves in favor of social poetry as it is understood by the older poets. Caludio Rodríguez and José Angel Valente take a different attitude; for them, poetry is a form of knowledge, as it is for Barral and Gil de Biedma, poets not included in the anthology. But while Rodríguez cannot be properly considered a social poet, Valente offers perhaps the best understanding of poetry's social function in contemporary society.

Among the commentaries about their works that each poet prepared for the anthology, "Conocimiento y comunicación" [Knowledge and Communication],[7] the essay by José Angel Valente is, undoubtedly, the most significant. Its author is the only poet of the period who was able to develop a coherent and aesthetically valid poetic theory and abide by it in his own work. Significantly enough, he opens with an epigraph by Louis Aragon, the French Surrealist poet who in the 1920s had set the foundations for a new conception of literature inspired by psychoanalysis and the belief in a deep, unconscious level of reality accessible through the poetic process:

La poésie me fait atteindre plus directement la realité, par une sorte de raccourci où surprend la clairière découverte. L'émotion poétique est le signe de la connaissance atteinte, de la conscience qui brûle les étapes.

(Poetry makes me attain reality in a more direct way, by means of a kind of short-cut where the uncovered glade surprises. The poetic emotion is the sign of the attained knowledge, of the unconsciousness that presses on.)

In his first paragraph Valente discredits the well-accepted idea that poetry is communication by the simple observation that it refers to "an effect that follows the creative poetic act, but that in no case alludes to the nature of the creative process." By focusing on the

poetic act, as Barral and Gil de Biedma had already done, the poet
can reach for the essence of poetry as a process, as a "means to the
knowledge of reality." Quite aware of the predictable criticism such
a conception would elicit from the supporters of a social function
of poetry, Valente underlines the fact that "even from a practical
point of view, and considering a contemporary defense of poetry,
the idea of poetry as knowledge offers a much more radical interest
than the theory of communication."

This last observation is of utmost importance for the development
of a new kind of social poetry in Spain, because it asks for a totally
different understanding of the poem's nature. Without denying the
communicative value of poetry, but setting it at the end of the
poetic process, and as an obvious consequence of it, Valente explains
that the primary function of poetry is to search for meaning in the
given reality: "Every poem is then an exploration into the material
of experience not known previously and that constitutes its object."
The poet has only one element to work with: language; and it is
through the effort to verbalize his experience of reality that the true
meaning of things comes to the fore. In other words, the poet
himself is the first one to receive knowledge from the poem he has
written.

Such a theory of poetic creation did not exclude the social value
of poetry, but only restated it in a more refined aesthetic conception,
in many ways related to a tradition temporarily obliterated by the
immediacy of the ideological fight and its demands for an effective
artistic weapon. The propagandistic art of the Fascist state was
counteracted by social poetry; considerations of style were mainly
a matter of clarity, purposefulness, and motivation. For José Angel
Valente and other poets of his age, the situation is totally different.

Having sought to restore to poetic language its power to give
meaning to reality, Valente began to write an analytical type of
poetry characterized by its essentiality, by a carefully conceived
structure, and by a stylistically "invisible" poem, that is, a text
deprived of almost all evidence of the rhetorical trappings of communicativeness. The contrast of his work in comparison to the
compositions written by authors like Celaya and Fuertes is so striking
that the two different coexistent types of social poetry emerge clearly.
Although the younger poets in general tend to be more careful about
the aesthetic aspect of their works, some did not write a totally new
form of poetry, but merely improved an already established style.

Attitudes toward the First Social Poets

The attitudes of the new poets toward the poetry of social criticism written by their elders vary from an enthusiastic recognition of its human and combative values to the criticism of its lack of profundity and its manifest antiaestheticism. This variety of responses is documented not only by the Ribes anthology, but also by the works of other poets not included in it. José Agustín Goytisolo represents one extreme in the spectrum. His poem "Los celestiales" [The Heavenly Ones][8] relates the story of the postwar poets in Spain, contrasting the formalist and religious preferences of the 1940s with the social tendency of the 1950s, which he embraces eagerly. In accordance with the characteristics of his other work, this composition is stylistically comparable to writings of the older poets, mainly because it tends to overdramatize the speaker's attitude and to lengthen the development of the poem. These aspects disappear in the works of the best contemporary poets.

In a simple and straightforward language with a markedly oral tone, the speaker makes ironical comments about the poets of the first postwar years:

> Después y por encima de la pared caída,
> de los vidrios caídos, de la puerta arrasada,
> cuando se alejó el eco de las detonaciones
> y el humo y sus olores abandonaron la ciudad,
> después, cuando el orgullo se refugió en las cuevas,
> mordiéndose los puños para no decir nada,
> arriba, en los paseos, en las calles con ruina
> que el sol acariciaba con sus manos de amigo,
> asomaron los poetas, gente de orden, por supuesto.

(Afterwards, and above the fallen wall, the fallen window panes, the smashed door, when the echo of the guns withered away, and the smoke and its smells abandoned the town; afterwards, when pride, biting its fists to avoid saying a word, looked for a refuge in the caves, above, in the parks and streets with ruins that the sun caressed with friendly hands, the poets appeared; they were people of order, of course.)

As in most of his compositions, Goytisolo seeks direct effect through a rhetoric of contrast and emphasis. In this stanza are seen the extremely long and convoluted period, the enumerative and repetitive nature of the structure, the different and not quite corresponding images, as well as the apparent change of attitude at the last moment. The same applies to the following stanza, in which another typical aspect of Goytisolo's work is also present—the overt use of ridiculing humor:

> Es la hora, dijeron, de cantar los asuntos
> maravillosamente insustanciales, es decir,
> el momento de olvidarnos de todo lo ocurrido
> y componer hermosos versos, vacíos, sí, pero sonoros,
> melodiosos como el laúd,
> que adormezcan, que transfiguren,
> que apacigüen los ánimos, ¡qué barbaridad!

(It is time, they said, to sing the wonderfully insubstantial subjects, that is to say, it is the moment to forget about what happened and to compose beautiful verses, empty verses, yes, but resounding, melodic like the lute; verses that would produce sleep, that would transfigure, that would calm the minds, what nonsense!)

His criticism against postwar poets touches also the religious poetry of the day, and the sarcasm is all too evident:

> Y así el buen Dios sustituyó
> al viejo padre Garcilaso, y fue llamado
> dulce tirano, amigo, mesías
> lejanísimo, sátrapa fiel, amante, guerrillero,
> gran parido, asidero de mi sangre, y los Oh, Tú,
> y los Señor, Señor, se elevaron altísimos, empujados
> por los golpes de pecho en el papel,
> por el dolor de tantos corazones valientes.

(And thus, the good God took the place of old father Garcilaso, and was called sweet tyrant, friend, remote Messiah, loyal satrap, lover, partisan, grand son of woman, handhold of my blood; and the Oh, You, and the Lord, Lord, lifted up high pushed up by penance on paper, by the pain of so many valiant hearts.)

The following and final stanza offers the contrast of social poetry; significantly in this case, there is no clear reference to the form, but only to the subject:

> Esta es la historia, caballeros,

> de los poetas celestiales, historia clara
> y verdadera, y cuyo ejemplo no han seguido
> los poetas locos, que, perdidos
> en el tumulto callejero, cantan al hombre,
> satirizan o aman el reino de los hombres,
> tan pasajero, tan falaz, y en su locura
> lanzan gritos, pidiendo paz, pidiendo patria,
> pidiendo aire verdadero.

(This is, gentlemen, the story of the heavenly poets, a clear and true story, an example that has not been followed by the crazy poets, the ones who, lost in the tumult of the streets, sing for man, satirize or love the kingdom of men, so fleeting, so deceptive, and in their madness they shout, asking for peace, asking for a motherland, asking for real air.)

Although brief, this last stanza summarizes several topics of social poetry as conceived by the proponents of poetry as *engagement,* a form of commitment to society through the direct communication with the masses. The social poet is immersed in the human activity of the street not only as an observer but also as a voice calling for attention. Goytisolo uses first the verb *cantar* ("to sing"), traditionally related to poetic diction, and immediately after, the expression *lanzar gritos* ("to shout") that applies preferably to the poetry of protest. None of these expressions describes the attitude of the younger poets, but they refer to the posture of Otero, Celaya, Fuertes, and the like.

When younger poets like González, Valente, Gil de Biedma, or Caballero Bonald go out to the street, as Otero and Celaya did, it is not to shout or to make demands for the masses. They come only as observers of the immediate reality, as analysts of their history, that is, the history of their people. Their function as poets is to expose reality to the naked eye, to make it visible in all its details. They do not sing in praise, they do not shout in anger: they simply describe what they see and discover around them. The difference with respect to the other attitude is evident in the tone of the voice and in the exactness of their language. The beginning of a poem by José Manuel Caballero Bonald expresses the interiorization of a commitment to social and political matters:

> Cuando estas palabras escribo
> sabiendo de antemano que jamás premio alguno

ni precaria mentira podrán mover mi boca,
sabiendo que estas páginas ondulan
como respiraciones de un dios inexorable
que va dando nivel y poderío a mi conciencia,
sabiendo, en fin, que cuantas verdades diga
han de ser sin remedio y vanamente,
entonces, el fundamento de mi propio vivir,
esa tierra de nadie en que me arraigo,
se junta a cuanto existe, lucha contra el asedio
del tiempo fementido y hace allí forjando
su mísera lección, creciendo
entre preguntas, irguiéndose entre ruinas,
hasta hacerse cenizas de mis propias palabras.

(When I write these words, knowing beforehand that never will any price or precarious lie move my mouth; knowing that these pages wave like the breathing of an inexorable god giving a level and power to my conscience; knowing, finally, that all the truth I might say will be irrevocable and vainly said; then, the foundation of my own life, this no one's land in which I am rooted, joins all existing matter, fights against the siege of treacherous time, and lies there, forging its miserable teaching, growing among questions, rising up among ruins, till it becomes ashes of my own words.)[9]

Equally emotional are the words of Valente in his poem "No mirar" [Not to Look]:

Escribo lo que veo,
aunque podría soñarlo
si no tuviera ojos para ver
y un reino de ceniza al alcance del viento,
si no estuviese en una jaula
aprisionado por mis ojos,
si mi reino no fuera de este mundo,
si no me apalearan
y me dieran también aceite y pan
para tapar los agujeros hondos de la muerte
con dolor compartido

(I write what I see, although I could dream it if I did not have eyes to see, and a kingdom of ashes at the reach of the wind, if I were not in a cage, imprisoned by my eyes, if my kingdom were not of this world, if they did not hit me and gave me also oil and bread to cover the deep holes of death with partaken pain.)[10]

But if their testimony does not take them to the public forum or require from them the dramatics of public speech, there are other points of contact with the older social poets. This is the case, for instance, with Valente's verse "if my kingdom were not of this world," an overt allusion to a biblical expression already used by other social poets, in particular by Blas de Otero. This verse is an example of his allusive technique of transforming a common or well-known expression for communicative purposes: to change Christ's phrase from a negative to an affirmative statement enhances the meaning of the allusive sentence. This technique became the model for other social poets and constitutes one of the characteristic procedures for poetic knowledge in Valente's work.[11] The reappearance of the same expression as well as the same technique in Valente's text indicates how social poets share a distinct set of terms, topics, and cross references that make of their works a somewhat coherent and interrelated body in spite of the notorious individual differences.

The references to Otero's work in Goytisolo's cited text evince his admiration for the older poet. Similar recognition has been accorded him and other poets of his age group by Angel González and José Manuel Caballero Bonald. In "Soneto a algunos poetas" [Sonnet to Some Poets], published in his first book, *Aspero Mundo* [Harsh World, 1956], González pays homage to his immediate predecessors, the poets whose works he read avidly in his youth:

> Todas vuestras palabras son oscuras.
> Avanzáis hacia el hombre con serena
> palidez: miedo trágico que os llena
> la boca de palabras más bien puras.
>
> Decís palabras sórdidas y duras:
> "fusil," "muchacha," "dolorido," "hiena."
> Lloráis a veces. Honda es vuestra pena.
> Oscura, inútil, triste entre basuras.
>
> España es una plaza provinciana
> y en ella pregonáis la mercancía:
> "un niño muerto por una azucena."
>
> Nadie se para a oíros. Y mañana

proseguiréis llorando. Día a día.
. . . Impura, inútil, honda es vuestra pena.

(All your words are dark. You walk toward man with serene paleness: tragic fear that fills your mouth with words that are rather pure. You say sordid and hard words: "rifle," "girl," "painfully," "hyena." Sometimes you cry. Deep is your sorrow: dark, useless, sad among the garbage. Spain is a provincial square, and you voice in it your merchandise: "a boy killed by a white lily." No one stops to listen. And tomorrow you will resume weeping. Day by day. . . . Impure, useless, deep is your sorrow.)[12]

Caballero Bonald's response to the first social poets is primarily that of a critic; he published a few articles about them, in which he praises the committed character of their works.[13] Valente, in turn, recognizes as a critic the preeminence of Otero, whom he considers "one of the poets of the first postwar promotion whose work offers more obvious interest."[14] But Valente is a harsh critic of the rest of the poets who followed the call for a socially committed poetry. In his article "Tendencia y estilo" [Trend and Style][15] Valente denounces the antiaestheticism of the social poets as a result of formalism in themes and trends. He sees among his contemporaries "the anomalous superabundance of the trend in grave detriment of the style." For him the main defect of the socially inspired poetry is that "Poets seem to be more interested in voicing certain themes than in discovering the truth of which these same themes could be the ideological statement."

A similar critical attitude pervades Carlos Barral's analysis of the evolution of Spanish poetry during the 1950s. In his article "Reflexiones acerca de las aventuras del estilo en la penúltima literatura española" [Reflections about the Adventures of the Style in the Next-to-Last Spanish Literary Period][16] he writes: "The so-called state of social poetry is, from the point of view that matters to us—that of the history of the literary techniques—a deplorable state." Like Valente, he sets aside consideration of poetry's subject matter to center his attention on the poetic language, on the techniques of literary creation, an aspect that had been considered too lightly, even disparagingly, by the proponents of an easily communicative verse.

The Art of Conciseness

The understanding of the poetic process as a form of knowledge affected deeply the whole conception of the poet, his social function, and his artistic endeavor. The most outstanding names in this second promotion of social poets could not conceive of themselves as anything but artists, that is, intellectuals whose main objectives were to achieve a more profound sense of understanding of themselves and of their world, and to make it available to others through poetic language. That was essentially their social duty, particularly because they were members of a profoundly unjust society that conformed to totally deceiving principles.

They believed, as José Angel Valente puts it in his poem of homage to Isidore Ducasse, that "Un poeta debe ser más útil / que ningún ciudadano de su tribu" ("A poet has to be more useful than any other member of his tribe.").[17] This is because "La poesía ha de tener por fin la verdad práctica." ("Poetry has to have practical truth as its aim"). In other words, they hoped for much more than the older social poets did, and they felt that poetry has an arduous mission: "Su misión es difícil" ("Its mission is difficult"), continues Valente's poem.

In effect, to get to the truth is not an easy matter, especially when the tool that must be used is language. The poets have no other means of reaching their aim, and consequently they cannot take language for granted. Each poem becomes a well-defined structure in which the concentration of techniques aims at an enriched meaning of words and expressions. The careful handling of the language at different levels—metaphoric, allusive, colloquial—is a trademark of these poets and defines their common style. If the older social poets express themselves in rhetorical and even bombastic terms and styles, the newer poets prefer the apparent simplicity of a condensed and restrained poem in which different forces create a tense mood conducive to meditation and interior views of reality.

Even accounting for the obvious differences due to individual stylistic traits, most of these poets show a preference for brevity and conciseness. The compositions they write are never too long and can be read in a few minutes or less; the structure of the poems is well centered around one subject, and leaves no room for elaborations or amplifications of any sort. The final text appears as a tightly enclosed unity, not always easy to penetrate. Even their complete works seem brief in comparison with the production common to most poets. Several factors made this economy of expression possible on the part of the younger social poets.

For one, the versification they use is rarely too noticeable; it is neither the very structured form of classical meters and stanzas, with the marked rhythm and rhyme, nor the striking novelties and experimental character of a totally free verse. Their poems are written in subtle combinations of traditional meters; in some cases they are very near blank verse, as in many poems by Jaime Gil de Biedma or in most of J. M. Caballero Bonald's compositions. In other cases, as in Angel González's and José Angel Valente's works, the meter is more varied and tries to follow the natural pauses and accents of the discourse.[18]

A comparison of different poems will give a better idea of the general tendency among these poets. Caballero Bonald's "Orbita de la palabra" [Orbit of the Word, *V.P.C.,* 20] is a poem in alexandrines:

> Yo he dicho, por ejemplo, amada, pueblo mío,
> madre mía, esperanza, somos iguales, siempre,
> pan, hermano, te quiero. He dicho, en fin, que el mundo,
> cabe en mis labios, gira en sus bordes, me dicta
> su dominio insaciable, me oprime entre los nudos
> que amordazan la historia furtiva de quien fui.

(I have said, for instance, lover, my people, my mother, hope, we are equal, always, bread, brother, I love you. I have said, finally, that the world fits in my lips, whirls in its borders, dictates its insatiable dominion, presses me in the knots that gag the furtive story of whom I was.)

Similarly, Gil de Biedma writes some compositions in stanzas as traditional as tercets:

> Mirad la noche del adolescente.
> Atrás quedaron las solicitudes
> del día, su familia de temores,
>
> y la distancia pasa en avenida
> de memorias o tumbas sin ciudad,

> arrabales confusos lentamente
>
> apagados. La noche se afianza
> —hasta los cielos cada vez, contigua
> la sien late en el centro.[19]

(Look at the night of the adolescent. Far back were left the day's solicitations, their family of fears, and distance passes in avenues of memory or tombs without a city, confusing outskirts slowly darkened. Night sets firmly—each time till the sky, near, the temple palpitates in the center.)

Both texts are patterned rhythmically like many other compositions in the history of Spanish poetry; they even make use of run-on verses and internal long pauses indicating the end of a sentence. To a great extent the effect of the poem depends precisely on this accepted model, in the cadence of the voice that follows the established meter. The same poets also combine different meters as insinuated by the last verse of the third stanza cited from the poem by Gil de Biedma. The combination is characteristic of Valente's highly structured texts; thus his poem "El corazón" [The Heart, *P.C.,* 21]:

> Ni una voz, ni un sonido
> conviviéndose en él.
> Si hundo mi mano extraigo
> sombra;
> si mi pupila,
> noche;
> si mi palabra,
> sed.

(Not a voice, not a sound living together in it. If I plunge in my hand I bring out shadows; if my eye, night; if my word, thirst.)

The metric structure of the composition is clearly determined by the content of the text, by its syntactical structure, and by an almost visual presentation of the three conditional sentences. Since Valente has a particular liking for parallelistic poetry, it is not rare to find many varieties of the main model in his poetry; these, of course, follow a metric presentation corresponding to the parallel structure of the syntactical, conceptual, and metaphorical levels.

Less dependent on previous models, Angel González combines different verse meters in his poems mainly to convey a sense of expressiveness through rhythm. Each verse indicates a measure of rhythm, a pause to be read. It is no coincidence that González's poetry is more emotional than that of Valente; his versification tries to make this emotion appear to the reader in the form of a clearly determined reading. Verses, and their positions inside the poem, become interpretative signs, like the exclamation mark or the instructions of a music score:

> A eso de las siete cruzó el cielo
> una lenta avioneta, y ni los niños
> la miraron.
>   Se desató
> el frío,
> alguien salió a la calle con sombrero,
> ayer, y todo el día
> fue igual,
> ya veis,
> qué divertido,
> ayer y siempre ayer y así hasta ahora,
> continuamente andando por las calles
> gente desconocida,
> o bien dentro de casa merendando
> pan y café con leche, ¡qué
> alegría!

(Around seven o'clock a small plane crossed the sky slowly, and not even the children looked at it. The cold came, somebody went out into the street wearing a hat, yesterday, and the whole day was the same, you see how much fun it was, yesterday and always yesterday and like this till today, always unknown people, walking the streets, or inside the house eating bread and drinking coffee and milk, such happiness!) (*P.S.P.*, 86)

The absence of full rhyme in all of the poems reinforces the unmarked quality of the style of these poets. Instead of the regular repetition of sounds, they prefer the subtler use of a few assonances, some interior rhymes, and other forms of resonance, like repetitions, parallelism, or even appropriation of expressions from common language or other sources well known by a large sector of the Spanish public. This is particularly true in the case of Valente, who, improving upon the technique already used by Blas de Otero, developed a complex system of allusions, paraphrases, repetitions, and echoes that make his work difficult for the careless reader.

A typical poem of this group should require from the reader the same type of effort that was demanded from the writers; conciseness is but the result of their search for truth, a search that implies also the appropriate expression of such truth. It must be noted here that the truth they were looking for was not limited to the political and social reality of contemporary Spain, but included a much wider understanding of man's destiny as an individual. Thus, many poems were devoted to other subjects not directly related to social matters; furthermore some of these poets wrote only a very few compositions that could be termed thoroughly social.

As said before, for them the social function of poetry does not imply a straightforward treatment of social subjects, neither does it demand direct expression of political views; what the poet can do for society is to search for a better understanding of man and society through language. Gil de Biedma puts it quite well in his "Arte poética" [Ars Poetica, *P.V.*, 37]:

> Es sin duda el momento de pensar
> que el hecho de estar vivo exige algo,
> acaso heroicidades—o basta, simplemente,
> alguna humilde cosa común
>
> cuya corteza de materia terrestre
> tratar entre los dedos, con un poco de fe?
> Palabras, por ejemplo.
> Palabras de familia gastadas tibiamente.

(Without doubt now is the moment to start thinking about the fact that being alive demands something, perhaps heroic acts—or does it suffice simply to touch with the fingers, with some faith, some humble common thing whose bark [is] of terrestrial matter? Words, for instance. Familiar words worn out warmly.)

The condensation of poetic language, of which this poem is a good example, is also achieved by the reduction of adjectival material, including comparisons and elaborate metaphors. These poets approve of symbolic and metaphoric language as long as it keeps a character of concreteness and opens a way for the correct interpretation of reality. Such is the case of several images used by most of them with nearly identical meaning. They not only coincide in a sense of style characterized by conciseness, but also partake of similar historical experiences leading them toward a common set of representations of the world they would like to decipher, understand, and transform.

Chapter Eight
Images of the World

The highly political years of the Republic, the traumatic experience of the Civil War, and the extremely disciplined society of postwar Spain could explain why, for so many contemporary Spaniards, politics and social matters became an always-present and compelling preoccupation. The children of this world of exacerbated political tensions grew highly sensitized to the social aspects of their circumstances and to their own dependence on an external reality they did not like and could not change. Spain had been dramatically shaken by its sociopolitical history, and the Franco regime—infatuated with Fascist myths of national destiny and historical tradition—insisted further in the preeminence of the nation and the collectivity over the consideration of individualism. It is understandable, then, that most of the poets born around the first years of increasing political turmoil saw the world with similar eyes and from a similar point of view—that of a socially conscious individual.

The personal circumstances for these poets were determined by their specific location—Spain, isolated from the rest of Europe—and by their times, represented by two main periods—the years of the Civil War, which they knew as children, and the oppressive first decades of Francoist peace. All of them lived through similar growing experiences during and after the war. While this one was their most impressive personal experience, their intellectual, moral, and emotional characters were molded by the long, more difficult years of adolescence and early youth, when they had to conform to the strict discipline and to the limited outlook of their Catholic schools and of the triumphal ideology of Nationalist Spain.[1]

The Collective Man

Both historical circumstances—war and the afterwar years—are seen by the young poets with the growing awareness that they were not alone in experiencing them, that their sadness and despair were

125

felt by many men in the same predicament. Of his early days as an aspiring poet, Angel González remembers: "The readings in those days of other poets—like Celaya, Hierro, de Nora—helped me understand that the writing of poetry could be something more than a simple personal expression, and that my pessimism and my tendency to melancholy did not come only from what we could call intimate affective dispositions, but that they were especially the result of a collective defeat, of a humiliation that overflowed the limits of individuality."[2]

Two ideas common to practically every social poet form the core of this text and reappear in several poems and commentaries. One is the realization that the individual is not alone, but surrounded by other men very much like himself; the other one, a consequence of the first, supports the conception of poetry as essentially social. The poet who talks about his own self is also talking about other men for the simple reason that they have a community of experience—they share the same world.

This sense of participation is found in several poems that discuss the historical experiences of a whole group in the first-person plural. José Angel Valente expresses it best in his composition "Patria, cuyo nombre no sé" [Fatherland, Whose Name I Do Not Know].[3] He combines the subject of Spain—a frequent topic with most postwar Spanish poets—with the historical fact of the war and the growing recognition of the communal destiny of most Spaniards. The poem opens with an emphatic first-person singular pronoun: "Yo no sé si te miro / con amor o con odio / ni si eres más que tierra / para mí." ("I do not know if I look at you with love or hatred, neither do I know if you are something more than earth for me").

For almost sixty lines the speaker, a young man, talks only about himself, about his being conditioned by his country and his time:

> Vine cuando la sangre
> aún estaba en las puertas
> y pregunté por qué.
> Yo era hijo de ella
> y tal sólo por esto
> capaz de ser en ti.

(I came when there was blood still on the doors, and I asked why. I was its offspring, and only because of that I was able to exist in you.)

In his characteristically brief and exact poetic style, Valente introduces the communal aspect, and the present state of the matter, with a change of pronoun—from singular to plural—and a change of tense; the location—Spain—is the same, as indicated by the verb "to come," which has a clearly demonstrative meaning: "Hemos venido. Estamos / solos. Pregunto, / ¿quién tiene tu verdad?" ("We have come. We are alone. I ask, who knows your truth?").

The final question expresses the need for knowledge that inspires most of Valente's poetry and that of his contemporaries. Such need leads them to review their immediate past, their memories of the days when they awoke to a world full of violence, death, and repression. And those memories are, in many cases, expressed also in the first-person plural, to stress the identification of all members in a generation. Caballero Bonald's poem "Primeras letras" [First Lessons][4] from his book *Pliegos de Cordel* [Popular Songs, 1963] ends also with a question addressed to Spain:

> Oh qué terribles y primeras
> letras letales
> de la patria. Párvula madre
> mía, ¿qué hiciste
> de nosotros, los que apenas
> pudimos aprender
> la tabla de sumar de la esperanza?

(Oh, such terrible and first lethal lessons of my country. Innocent mother, what did you do with us, the ones who barely could learn the addition rules of hope?)

In both poems the first-person-plural pronoun indicates the shared historical experience of a promotion; the final questions, in turn, refer to the poet's realization of his social duty, this is, the need to know the truth about his world, a world in which he is not alone. Being a poet means being able to speak for everyone, being, in other words, the voice of the people. And this is possible mainly because the poet sees himself as identical to the rest of men; he is not different from anyone.

The identification with other persons, with all of humanity, is obviously a paramount characteristic of social poetry. It takes other manifestations besides the first-person-plural pronoun, appearing

directly expressed, for instance, in "Todo lo que he vivido" [All I
Have Lived], a poem by Caballero Bonald:

> Desde mi propio miedo, desde
> la libertad de estar viviendo, desde el fondo
> de mí, que soy igual que todos,
> que aprendo igual que todos a rescatar el tiempo,
> traigo mi voz y su holocausto,
> la diaria historia de mis conjeturas,
> para que no esté sola mi palabra,
> para poder vivir quizá
> desde el merecimiento en que la creo.

(From my own fear, from the freedom of being alive, from the depths of
myself, because I am equal to everyone, and learn like anyone to recuperate
time, I bring my voice and its holocaust, the daily story of my conjectures,
so that the word be not alone, so that I might live in the merit I think
it has.) (*V.P.C.*, 24–25)

This stanza, which also communicates the sense of belonging that
motivates the poet to write, is part of a longer poem in which the
speaker addresses a collective, undetermined group of readers, thus
stressing the idea of communal interrelation:

> Todo lo que he vivido, todo
> lo que he salvado vigilantemente
> del feroz exterminio de los días,
> todo cuanto yo fui, hoy os lo ofrezco,
> ojos que seguiréis el rastro de estas letras,
> pechos que olvidaréis mi reducción del mundo,
> mi modo de vivir, todo os lo doy ahora
> lo mismo que os daría mi palabra final
> en su declinación de certidumbre única.

(All I have lived, all I have saved, attentively, from the ferocious exter-
mination of the days, all that I was, I offer today to you, eyes that will
follow the trace of these letters, chests that will forget my reduction of
the world, my way of living, I give you everything now, as I would give
you my last word in its declension of the only certitude.)

The addressed second-person plural can become one and the same
entity with that designated by the first-person plural, as seen in

"Amistad a lo largo" [A Long-Lived Friendship], a poem by Jaime Gil de Biedma:

> Pasan lentos los días
> y muchas veces estuvimos solos.
> Pero luego hay momentos felices
> para dejarse ser en amistad.
> > > > > > Mirad:
> somos nosotros.

(The days pass slowly and many times we were lonely. But then there are happy moments to let oneself be in friendship.)[5]

The poems about friendship bring a stronger feeling of the community of experience, because they consider it from a point of view more emotional and true to life than the generalizations of political poems which equate community of experience with anonymous masses. Gil de Biedma portrays the actual fact of growing together:

> Un destino condujo diestramente
> las horas, y brotó la compañía.
> Llegaban noches. Al amor de ellas
> nosotros encendíamos palabras.,
> las palabras que luego abandonamos
> para subir a más:
> empezamos a ser los compañeros
> que se conocen
> por encima de la voz o de la seña.

(A destiny led the hours deftly, and companionship sprang. Nights came. By their hearth we lighted words, the words that later we left aside in order to climb higher: we began to be the companions who know each other beyond their voices or their gestures.)

In what it has of communal sharing, friendship represents a human value, a manifestation of man's capacity for love and caring. In friendship the individual finds a sense of belonging, a support against life's vicissitudes. Friends talk to each other about their lives and, through their shared experiences, reach an understanding of themselves and their world:

Quiero deciros cómo todos trajimos
nuestras vidas aquí, para contarlas.
Largamente, los unos con los otros
en el rincón hablamos, tantos meses!
que nos sabemos bien, y en el recuerdo
el júbilo es igual a la tristeza.
Para nosotros el dolor es tierno.

Ay el tiempo! Ya todo se comprende.

(I want to tell you how all of us brought up our lives here to tell them. Lengthily we talk to each other in the corner, so many months that we know each other very well, and in memory joy is identical to sadness. For us, pain is tender. Ah, time! All is now understood.)

The poet is like a friend recounting his personal story to the rest of men, aiming to find a meaning of value to all. As Gil de Biedma puts it in the introduction to his book *Compañeros de viaje* [Fellow Travelers, 1959], "After all, a book of poems is nothing but the story of a man who is its author, raised to a level of meaning in which the life of one man is the life of all men, or at least . . . of several among them" (*P.V.,* 16). The realization that one man's life is no different from the lives of his fellow men, and particularly of those who belong with him in the same time and place, is the basis of the social poet's interest in autobiographical accounts; it also justifies his tendency to write narrative poems about other people's lives.

Memories of the Past

Several are the compositions in which these young poets remember their boyhood and adolescence; born in the second half of the 1920s, all of them were only boys at the outset of the Civil War in the summer of 1936. For J. M. Caballero Bonald the Civil War meant the sudden end of his summer vacation. In "La llave" [The Key, *V.P.C.,* 220–22], he narrates how his family arrived at the summer home and how he was given the key to a room where he could have his laboratory, "all the materials with which I experimented my nine-year-old freedom." But the perfectly ideal world of boyhood disappears when the war comes:

> Dueño del cuarto,
> con la llave amarrada a mi cadena
> de hombre, cómo me convencía
> de ser más justo entre los ilusorios
> oficios de azufre, cuando el sol
> de la iracunda siesta
> cegaba el trajinar de lo diario.
>
> Mi posesión de tanta vida,
> mi heredad de probetas, ¿dónde
> se fueron cuando el dieciocho
> de julio de aquel año
> tuvimos que volver a la ciudad?

(Lord of my room, with the key tied to my man's chain, how I assured myself of being more just among the illusory works of sulphur, when the sun of the raging nap blinded the daily activities. My possessions of so much life, my inheritance of test tubes, where did they go when on July eighteenth of that year we had to return to town?)

The images of war are reduced, quite sensibly, to the limited perspective of the boy who only hears, from inside the house, the noises of battle, and sees fear in the frightened reactions of the grown-ups:

> Detrás de los cristales, escuchaba
> los primeros disparos, el temible
> golpear de las puertas
> del coche celular y, sobre todo,
> los pasos de mi madre, resonando
> entre las vetas de lo oscuro
> cada vez que un motor
> destazaba su furia en los balcones.

(From behind the windows I could hear the first shots, the fearful slamming of the army car doors, and, above all, the steps of my mother, resounding in the shades of darkness each time an engine cut up its fury in the balconies.)

In general, none of the poets in this group lingers upon detailed visions of the war itself; the conflict is mostly alluded to briefly, as if avoiding its ugliness. In his poem "Autobiografía" [Autobiography],[6] José Agustín Goytisolo makes a very short reference to the war:

> Vino, luego, la guerra,
> la muerte—yo la vi—
> y cuando hubo pasado
> y todos la olvidaron,
> yo, triste, seguí oyendo:
> no sirves para nada.

(Then, the war came, death—I saw it—and when it had passed and everybody had forgotten it, I, sad, continued listening: you are good for nothing.)

The brief parenthetical comment, with its directness, is enough to convey the idea of having experienced the pains and sadness of the war. There is no need to stress the concreteness of details that could only coarsen the poetic expression; thus, when Angel González mentions the days of the war, he uses metaphoric language: "A long time ago I was a boy and it snowed and snowed."[7]

Time—related to seasons, months, and days, and to its three dimensions, past, present, and future—pervades all of González's work, the image of winter signifying the bad times of the war, and also the long period of postwar dictatorship. The poem "Diciembre" [December, *P.S.P.*, 94–95], constitutes an extended image of winter, defeat, and sorrow for what has been lost; the contrast between winter and the previous season underlines the sad differences:

> Diciembre vino así, como lo cuento
> aquel año de gracia del que hablo,
> el año aquel de gracia y sueño, leve
> soplo de luces y de días,
> encrucijada luminosa
> de lunas hondas y de estrellas altas,
> de mañanas de sol, de tardes tibias
> que por el aire se sucedían lentas
> como globos brillantes y solemnes.
>
> Pero diciembre vino de ese modo
> y cubrió todo aquello de ceniza:
> lluvia turbia y menuda,
> niebla densa,
> opaca luz borrando los perfiles,
> espeso frío tenaz que vaciaba

las calles de muchachas
y de música,
que asesinaba pájaros y mármoles
en la ciudad sin hojas del invierno.

(So, December came, as I say, that year of our Lord of which I am talking about; that year of our Lord and dream, light blow of lights and days, luminous criss-cross of deep moons and high stars, of sunny mornings, warm afternoons that succeeded each other in the air, slowly, like great and solemn balloons. But December came in that way and covered everything with ashes: dark and soft rain, dense fog, dull light erasing the profiles of things, thick and stubborn cold that emptied the streets of girls and music, that murdered birds and marble in the leafless city of winter.)

Before winter it was summer, it was the beautiful time of yesterday, now gone:

Te tuve
cuando eras
dulce,
acariciado mundo.
Realidad casi nube,
¡cómo te me volaste de los brazos!

(I had you, when you were sweet, caressed world. Reality, almost a cloud, how did you fly away from my embrace! (*P.S.P.,* 11)

Boyhood can very easily be equated with a time of paradisiacal beauty, when there is no conscience of the world's imperfections, and the individual feels totally immersed in an ideal reality. It seems natural, then, that these poets feel as if they have been deprived of something that rightly belonged to them.

The subject of childhood is central to Carlos Sahagún's poetry.[8] The grown man cannot forget that he was a boy stricken by harsh reality: "And I know that the man who lived as a boy in Almería will never be able to forget that dark presence of suffering, the first experience of his life."[9] The adjective "dark" and the use of "night" in the title of his collected poems—*Memorial de la noche* [Night's Memorial]—are in accordance with Sahagún's easily understandable system of symbols, as well as with the repeated use of the opposites "light" and "darkness" in most of the social poets. The poems by Caballero Bonald and González are examples of the well-defined contrast applied to signify the two world of pre- and postwar Spain.

Types of Imagery

The social poet's fondness for simple, well-accepted images is largely due to a need for both a clarity of expression and a poetic disguise of the discourse. Well-known images also work in resonance with various accepted meanings, thus enriching the communicative value of the poem. Essential for the effectiveness of the method is the appropriate combination of different allusive elements in the poem. In a composition that summarizes the topic of the lost happiness of boyhood, Carlos Sahagún combines several common images to express the overwhelming sense of loss brought about by the triumph of the Nationalists. The poem, though, is not entirely effective because its structure and language are somewhat vague and verbose.[10]

The opening stanza could be read in different ways, either as a happy memory of school or as an ironical comment on the first postwar "years of peace." In any case, the image of water is less than significant:

> En el principio, el agua
> abrió todas las puertas, echó las campanas al vuelo,
> subió a las torres de la paz—eran tiempos de paz—,
> bajó a los hombros de mi profesor
> —aquellos hombros suyos tan metafísicos,
> tan doctrinales, tan
> florecidos de libros de Aristóteles—,
> bajó a sus hombros, no os engaño
> y saltó por su pecho como un pájaro vivo.

(At the beginning, water opened the doors, rang the bells, climbed the towers of peace—they were times of peace—, descended to the shoulders of my teacher—those shoulders of his, so metaphysic, so doctrinal, so flowery of Aristotle's books—, descended to his shoulders, I do not lie to you, and jumped on his chest like a lively bird.)

The image of water reappears a few verses later, this time referring perhaps to a period before the war; the paradisiacal aspect of that world is made evident:

> cuando el diluvio universal,
> el llanto universal,
> y un cielo todavía universal,
> el agua contraía matrimonio con el agua,
> y los hijos del agua eran pájaros, flores, peces, árboles;
> eran caminos, piedras, montañas, humo estrellas.

(When the universal deluge, the universal cry, and a sky that was still universal, water married water and the offspring of water were the birds, flowers, fish, trees; were the roads, stones, mountains, smoke, stars.)

Even at the end of the poem the symbol of water remains undecipherable:

> Aquello era la vida,
> era la vida y empujaba,
>   pero,
> cuando entraron los lobos, después, despacio, devorando,
> el agua se hizo amiga de la sangre,
> y en cascadas de sangre cayó, como una herida,
> cayó sobre los hombres
> desde el pecho de Dios, azul, eterno.

(That was life, it was life and pushed up, but, when the wolves came in, afterwards, slowly, eating, water became friendly with blood and fell in cascades of blood, like a wound, fell over men from the chest of God, blue, eternal.)

The symbol of water, much used by Sahagún in his poems, carries too many possible meanings and references to be effective if not made more specific. The language of clarity and disguise can easily stumble into inanity. In the case of this poem there is also a confusing organization and only the topical character of the subject makes it partially understandable.

In comparison with this poem, José Angel Valente's "Tiempo de guerra" [War Times, *P.C.,* 199–80] appears as an extremely clear, even too direct, composition. Although Valente does not necessarily avoid symbolic images in his works, in this text there is a total absence of them; but the language of the poem can be read on two levels, as in the case of González's verse about snowing, that refers both to actual snow, and to the metaphorical representation of postwar Spain. Irony is one of the favored poetic devices for Valente; he requires from his reader some form of participation—an ability to read beneath the surface.

The first stanza introduces two basic formulas in social poetry—the use of the first-person plural and the direct address to a group of readers or listeners; irony is already present in the attitude of the speaker, who makes a colloquial reference to an indefinite "they," felt as superior to the ones involved in the "situation" of the poem: "Estábamos, señores, en provincias / o en la periferia, como dicen, / incomprensiblemente desnacidos." ("Gentlemen, we were in the provinces, or, as they say, in the periphery, inexplicably unborn").

Those addressed are not the friends of Gil de Biedma's poems or the common people to whom the social poet looks for a response, but some "sclerotic gentlemen" who represent both old age and the political hardening of nationalism. Instead of using the naive images of "wolves" and "pigeons" seen in Sahagún's poem, Valente depicts truth in slightly deforming lines, as in a caricature: "Los niños con globitos colorados, / pantalones azules / y viernes sacrosantos / de piadoso susurro." ("The kids had little red balloons, blue trousers, and holy Fridays of pious murmurs").

The tense situation of the war behind the lines appears in concrete images, as if seen by the eye of an undiscerning boy; the mere superimposition of a few glimpses of reality reproduces well the scene and its colorful vivacity:

> Andábamos con nuestros
> papás.
>   Pasaban trenes
> cargados de soldados a la guerra.
> Gritos de excomunión.
>   Escapularios.
> Enormes moros, asombrosos moros
> llenos de pantalones y de dientes.
> Y aquel vertiginoso
> color del tíovivo y de los víctores.

(We walked with our fathers. Trains loaded with soldiers passed by toward the war. Shouts of excommunication. Scapularies. Huge Moors, astonishing Moors all trousers and teeth. And that vertiginous color of the merry-go-round and the hurrahs.)

The composition ends with a stanza in which the tone and attitude of the speaker are markedly critical; what begins with a seemingly humoristic enumeration, with repetition, ends in a sudden, unexpected verse of bitter judgment:

> Estábamos remotos
> chupando caramelos,
> con tantas estampitas y retratos
> y tanto ir y venir y tanta cólera,
> tanta predicación y tantos muertos
> y tanta sorda infancia irremediable.

(We were remote, licking lollipops, with so many religious prints and portraits, and so many ups and downs and so much ire, so many sermons and so many dead and so much of a dull and hopeless infancy.)

Directness and conciseness are not only Valente's qualities; they are also characteristic of other social poets who seek the piercing ironic phrase, the expressive contrast that needs no more elaboration and does not require the techniques of symbolic representations. When they do use symbols or metaphorical language, these function also at the concrete level of the reality depicted by the poem. Particularly devoid of any form of imagery is Gil de Biedma's poem "Intento formular mi experiencia de la guerra" [I Try to Explain My Experience of the War, *P.V.,* 119–21], which, as the title already insinuates, combines an analytical attitude with a reminiscent tone.

Gil de Biedma's style is at the opposite extreme of Sahagún's. While the latter depends greatly upon a rhetorical conception of poetry as the language of adornment and sentimentality, Gil de Biedma prefers to think of poetry as a restrained discourse in which there is no room for figurative language. The pathos of the poem has to come from the well-balanced interrelation between the emotional and the intellectual aspects of the speaker's voice. It is symptomatic of his style that he conceives the lyrical situation as a very close relation between speaker and listener. As indicated earlier, friendship defines the tone of Gil de Biedma's poems, the soft-spoken quality of the speaker's conversation.

In his memories of the war there are no other images than those of the world around:

> Para empezar, la guerra
> fue conocer los páramos con viento,
> los sembrados de gleba pegajosa
> y las tardes de azul, celestes y algo pálidas,
> con los montes de nieve sonrosada a lo lejos.

(To begin with, war was the knowledge of the windy barren plateaus, the sown fields of sticky soil, and the blue afternoons, sky blue and somewhat pale afternoons with the mountains of softly pink snow in the distance.)

Like Valente, he remembers a period of colorful political rallies, adding a more explicit analysis of his situation as a boy:

> Y los mismos discursos, los gritos, las canciones
> eran como promesas de otro tiempo mejor,
> nos ofrecían
> un billete de vuelta al siglo diez y seis.
> Qué niño no lo acepta?

(And the speeches, the shouts, the songs were like promises of a better time; they offered us a return ticket to the sixteenth century. What boy does not accept it?)

For him the war years "Fueron, posiblemente, / los años más felices de mi vida, / y no es extraño, puesto que al fin de cuentas / no tenía los diez" ("Those were perhaps the best years of my life, and it is not so strange because, after all, I was not ten years old yet"). But they were happy only because he was mistaken or was fooled by the circumstances. This feeling of having been deceived by their elders, by the whole of society, appears clearly in all of the poets commented upon, and provokes the ethical and intellectual attitude of these poets in the years following their adolescence. As Gil de Biedma says when finishing the poem, they did not discover truth until much later:

> Cuando por fin volvimos
> a Barcelona, me quedó unos meses
> la nostalgia de aquello, pero me acostumbré.
> Quien me conoce ahora
> dirá que mi experiencia

> nada tiene que ver con mis ideas,
> y es verdad. Mis ideas de la guerra cambiaron
> después, mucho después
> de que hubiera empezado la postguerra.

(When we finally returned to Barcelona, I had for a while nostalgic memories of that, but I got used to the new situation. Those who know me now will say that my experience has nothing to do with my ideas, and it is true. My ideas about the war changed later, much later after the postwar had begun.)

The Postwar Years

It was during the postwar period, when the young social poets grew up and matured, that they realized fully that they were living in an unjust society, that they were the victims of a system repressive of spontaneous manifestations of human freedom and creativity, totally contemptuous of individual human rights. It comes as no surprise that they adopted radical views on matters of politics, views that encompassed mainly the conviction of a need for a future betterment of Spanish circumstances through social and political reform. Their images of contemporary Spain are grim yet expectant.

As already commented, for Angel González winter symbolizes perfectly well his conception of postwar society: "El invierno / de lunas anchas y pequeños días / está sobre nosotros." ("Winter, with its wide moons and its short days, is upon us").[11] But winter is not a definitive state; its temporal nature stresses the political conviction in a future transformation of present reality into a better one—from winter to spring:

> Es increíble: pero todo esto
> que hoy es tierra dormida bajo el frío,
> será mañana, bajo el viento,
> trigo.
> > Y rojas
> amapolas. Y sarmientos . . .

(It is incredible: but all of this, that now is only a sleeping soil under the cold, tomorrow, under the wind, will be wheat. And red poppies. And vine shoots . . .)

The poem closes with a stanza in which the words forming the title of the book reappear—*Sin esperanza, con convencimiento* [Without

Hope, with Conviction, 1961]. Hope is also left aside in José Valente's *A modo de esperanza* [As If It Were Hope, 1955], a first book in which the barren aspects of Spanish life during the Franco years are represented, quite expressively, by the wide, endless emptiness of a desert. " 'Serán ceniza. . . .' " ["They Will Be Ashes," *P.C.*, 13] is an allegorical poem that describes well not only the poet's personal attitude toward the circumstances, but also those of his contemporaries. The language of disguise allows again for different levels of reading; but unlike Sahagún's poem, Valente's has a well-conceived structure, and the techniques of allusion are much more effective. In fact, the poem provides an excellent example of Valente's characteristic use of resonance:

> Cruzo un desierto y su secreta
> desolación sin nombre.
> El corazón
> tiene la sequedad de la piedra
> y los estallidos nocturnos
> de su materia o de su nada.

(I cross a desert and its secret and nameless desolation. The heart has the dryness of stone and the nocturnal blast of its matter or its nothingness.)

On a first, immediate level, these verses could be interpreted as an individual's conception of life as emptiness and solitude. The image of the *homo viator* would stress the idea of a spiritual journey in a dead world. This pessimistic outlook could be seen from another point of view if the reader relates this individual's situation with that of his contemporaries and observes the same impression of loneliness, sterility, and darkness in their works.

Valente's poem continues with a stanza that defines the social attitude of his age group:

> Hay una luz remota, sin embargo,
> y sé que no estoy solo;
> aunque después de tanto y tanto no haya
> ni un solo pensamiento
> capaz contra la muerte,
> no estoy solo.

(But there is a remote light, and I know, then, that I am not alone; even though after so much and so much there is no one thought capable of defeating death, I am not alone.)

The images used are related to the whole allegorical picture of the journey: they have a concrete visual value, and they also glow with enlarged auras of meaning because they belong to a traditional set of representations. The light in this case represents some hope in the form of another human being; the value of participation, of belonging to a human group is stressed further by the phrase "I am not alone."

But light in this poem does not necessarily mean only the presence of another human being. In Valente's work, as well as in that of other social poets, the opposition between light and darkness, day and night, is stereotyped. "Night" represents, as do "desert" and "winter," the ideological backwardness, the political dictatorship, the social injustice, the inhuman basis of Fascist Spain. There is nothing beautiful or magic in night; light, on the other hand, represents the opposite values of freedom, knowledge, social justice, humanitarianism, that will have to come, as spring comes after winter and day after night. That is why light is represented sometimes as dawn:

> He de llegar contigo a la alegría.
> Dame la mano, empuja mi corazón. Ahora
> sé que no estaba escrito todo, que hay una aurora
> sobre el vivir del hombre y alumbra todavía.

(I have to reach happiness with you. Give me your hand, push my heart. Now I know that not everything was written, that there is a dawn in man's life and light still gleams.)[12]

In Angel González's vision, dawn is directly related to the poet's ability to bring changes in the world, in spite of the barrier of silence surrounding him:

> Y luego,
> tras el instante enorme del silencio,
> cuando la tarde se convierta en sombra,
> verás brillar contra los imprecisos

> pabellones lejanos
> la roja luz, reflejo de tu aurora.

(And later, after the moment of intense silence, when the afternoon transforms itself into darkness, you will see shining against the blurred and far-away flags the red light, the reflection of your dawn.) (*P.S.P.*, 119)

The same conception of dawn as related to the poet's commitment to the social cause is present in "Primer poema" [First Poem], which introduces Valente's second book, *Poemas a Lázaro* [Poems for Lázaro, 1961]:

> Poeta, oh no,
> sujeto de una vieja impudicia:
> mi historia debe ser olvidada,
> mezclada en la suma total
> que la hará verdadera.
> Para vivir así,
> para ser así anónimamente
> reavivada y cambiada,
> para que el canto, al fin,
> libre de la aquejada
> mano, sea sólo poder,
> poder que brote puro
> como un gallo en la noche,
> como en la noche, súbito,
> un gallo rompe a ciegas
> el escuadrón compacto de las sombras.

(Poet, oh never, subject of an old indecency: my story has to be forgotten, mingled in the total sum that will make it truthful. In order to live like this, to be thus anonymously revitalized and changed, so that the song, finally, freed from the suffering hand, be only solely power, power that springs up pure like a rooster at night, like at night, suddenly a rooster breaks blindly the compact battalion of shadows.) (*P.C.*, 63–64)

The obvious allusion to the "socialist dawn" is appropriately complemented by the self-criticism of an individualist who has turned away from his previous egotistical and nihilist views of himself and humankind to partake in the common life of all men. Similar are the poems in which other young poets look with critical eyes at their bourgeois upbringing and conceptions of the world.

The Public Square

The ethical conflict between the individualism of the middle-class poet and his desire for a commitment to the cause of social reform is certainly an important aspect in the motivation to write social poetry. In the same way that Blas de Otero makes of his personal evolution—from religious existentialism to a social commitment—a subject for his poetry, the younger poets in the second promotion use their own experience to show to all those who belong to their class the way for a correct and desirable action. Their social poetry, then, is not precisely directed toward the lower classes, which, after all do not normally read poetry; it is the poetry of an economically and culturally privileged group, many of whose social equals need reeducation in matters of social consciousness.

Jaime Gil de Biedma represents the extreme attitude of displeasure and rejection of a social status that was once defended militarily and was violently maintained in Spain during the postwar years. In carefully constructed poems he evokes a period of careless social injustice, and a mood of moral decadence in the Spanish bourgeoisie:

> Mi infancia eran recuerdos de una casa
> con escuela y despensa y llave en el ropero,
> de cuando las familias
> acomodadas,
>   como su nombre indica,
> veraneaban infinitamente
> en *Villa Estefanía* o en *La Torre*
> *del Mirador*
>   ya más allá continuaba el mundo
> con senderos de grava y cenadores
> rústicos, decorado de hortensias pomposas,
> todo ligeramente egoísta y caduco.
> Yo nací (perdonadme)
> en la edad de la pérgola y el tenis.

(My infancy were memories of a house with a school and a pantry, with locks on the dressers; a house of a time when the comfortable families, as their name shows, used to spend the summers in *Villa Estefanía* or *La Torre del Mirador,* and farther away the world continued in gravel paths and rustic gazebos, decorated with pompous hydrangeas, and everything was slightly egotistic and decadent. I was born [and please forgive me] in the period of pergolas and tennis.) (*P.V.,* 47)

In "Barcelona ja no és bona, o mi paseo solitario en primavera" [Barcelona Is No Longer Any Good, or My Lonely Walk in Spring, *P.V.*, 77–79), the city brings him memories of his rich parents enjoying the avenues and parks, dining at the outdoor restaurants of the once-elegant Barcelona. Mingled with the reminiscence there is the feeling of guilt:

> Y a la nostalgia de una edad feliz
> y de dinero fácil, tal como la contaban,
> se mezcla un sentimiento bien distinto
> que aprendí de mayor,
>   este resentimiento
> contra la clase en que nací . . .

(And to the nostalgic memories of a happy age and of easy money, as they told us about it, is added another, very different feeling that I learned when I reached maturity—this resentment against the class into which I was born . . .)

In contrast to the private gardens and the area of fashionable avenues and restaurants, every city has another place that serves to symbolize the people jointly together, a recognition of their communal identity and destiny—the public square. Several social poets have written compositions in which this concrete image is used to refer to man's social condition and to the particular situation of Spain under the dictatorial postwar government.

Vicente Aleixandre, the master poet from the Generation of 1927, uses the image of the public square to represent the greatness of human solidarity that is the central theme in his book *Historia del corazón* [History of the Heart, 1954]. From the poem "En la plaza" [At the Public Square][13] come these verses that contain also the images of "light," "wind," and "hand," with a significance comparable to that found in other social poets:

> Era una gran plaza abierta, y había olor de
>   existencia.
> Un olor a gran sol descubierto, a viento rizándolo,
> un gran viento que sobre las cabezas pasaba su mano,
> su gran mano que rozaba las frentes unidas y las
>   reconfortaba.

(It was a large open plaza, and there was the fragrance of life. A smell of great open sun, of the wind that curled it, a great wind that passed its hand over the heads, its large hand that touched the united foreheads and comforted them.)

In accordance with the tone of the book as a whole, the speaker's attitude is that of one enthralled with the happiness and greatness of being at one with the rest of men. The too evident repetition of the adjective *gran* is indicative of the poet's intention to underline the importance of this matter, its cosmic character. Three initial verses combine repetition and enumeration to convey the emotion of being one with all: "Hermoso es, hermosamente humilde y confiante, vivificador y profundo, / sentirse bajo el / sol, entre los demás, impelido, / llevado, conducido, mezclado, rumorosamente arrastrado." ("It is beautiful, beautifully humble and entrusting, enlivening and profound, to feel oneself under the sun, among the rest of men, driven, carried, led, mingled, buzzingly washed away").

From the conviction of the superiority of the group over the individual, the poet derives the drive and enthusiasm to urge others to go into the square and be themselves in unity with all of mankind: "Así, entra con pies desnudos. Entra en el hervor, en la plaza." ("Like this, enter with naked feet. Get into the noise and upsurge of the waters, into the square"). Aleixandre's conception is vaguely related to the truly social attitude and convictions of the younger poets; for him, the community of all men is a poetic truth that finds its roots in his old views of reality as a unified form of cosmic existence. This is not precisely the social attitude of the younger poets, although it calls for the same urgent change from individualism to solidarity.

The public square, where all men meet and mingle in everyday social life, or rally in ceremonies and political gatherings, is the best representation of society's essence. Aleixandre feels and understands this essential communal quality of man's existence, and sees it symbolically in the throbbing square, filled with people. The younger poets have a different view, since they see in the square not only the concrete representation of the social body but also Spain's political and social repressions. That is why the poems in which they present the square contain a common insistence upon contrasting the present moment with a time when things were quite different.

J. M. Caballero Bonald in "Plaza Mayor" [Main Square, *V.P.C.*, 217–19] remembers his days as a student in Madrid, when he stopped going to the Main Square because someone told him that "they" were not coming anymore:

> ¿Quién, con tanta fraudulenta
> renuncia, me quería
> cegar (no lo recuerdo), quién
> y por qué me dijo que ya
> no volveríamos? *¿No ves*
> *la mugre delatora, el ceño*
> *municipal, la dirección*
> *prohibida?* . . .

(Who wanted to blind me with such cheating renunciation [I do not remember], who told me, and why, that we would not come back? *Don't you see the denouncing filth, the municipal brow, the forbidden direction?*) "Forbidden direction" also means "one-way street."

His conviction of the strength of his ideas inspires the closing verses of the poem, which assert that someday he will return to the Main Square; this faith in a future is similar to the one expressed in the certainty of dawn coming after night: "y volveré / cada día, / hasta aprenderme de memoria / los andenes del pueblo." ("And I will return each day until I have learned by heart the walkways of the people").

Not all of the younger social poets sound as hopeful as does Caballero Bonald. Jaime Gil de Biedma, for instance, relates the image of the square to the figure of a defeated republican. Using a technique also found in Valente's poems, his composition's speaker is an identifiable character, totally different from the poet. In "Piazza del Popolo" (*P.V.*, 68–70), the speaker is the Spanish intellectual María Zambrano, who remembers a political rally in the Square of the People:

> Del silencio,
> por encima de la plaza,
> creció de repente un trueno
> de voces juntas. Cantaban.
> Y yo cantaba con ellos.
> Oh sí, cantábamos todos

otra vez, qué movimiento,
qué revolución de soles
en el alma! Sonrieron
rostros de muertos amigos
saludándome a lo lejos
borrosos—pero qué jóvenes,
qué jóvenes sois los muertos!—
y una entera muchedumbre
me prorrumpió desde dentro
toda en pie. Bajo la luz
de un cielo puro y colérico
era la misma canción
en las plazas de otro pueblo,
era la misma esperanza,
el mismo latido inmenso
de un solo ensordecedor
corazón a voz en cuello.

(From silence, above the square, a thunder of joint voices grew suddenly. They sang. And I was singing with them. Oh yes, we all sang again, what movement, what a revolution of suns in the soul! Faces of dead friends blurred in the distance smiled calling me—but how young, how young you are my dead friends!—and a complete crowd burst inside of me and stood up. Under the light of a pure and irate sky, it was the same song in the squares of another people, it was the same hope, the same vast throb of an only and deadening heart shouting.)

Both sadness of defeat and hope for the future intermingle in the speaker's emotion; the strength of the political conviction, the force that from the group inspires the individual to act are still there, but mainly as a memory of the past, as a nostalgic remembrance of passionate days of political activism. For Angel González, a poet who has not known those days and walks the Main Square during the time of the dictatorship, the state of mind is somehow sadder and less optimistic:

Como un estanque sucio,
el tiempo
cubrió con su agua turbia las palabras,
los discursos, las frases
cargadas de propósitos sinceros.
Hubo más que palabras, ciertamente.

> Pero ahora
> sólo quedan los muros,
> impasibles testigos de esa historia
> y de otras muchas más,
> también pasadas.

(Like a dirty pool, time covered with its dark waters the words, the speeches, the phrases that carried sincere good intentions. There was more than words, certainly. But today only the walls remain, impassive witnesses of that history and of many others also passed.)[14]

This rebellious attitude seems possible only as a desire, not even a hope. Social poets of this second group are, in a way, less confident of a future change and express more openly their disillusionment:

> Y sin embargo,
> cuánta voz gritaría si pudiese,
> cuánta sangre
> —menos odiosa que esta indiferencia—
> mancharía de rojo las paredes.

(But then, how many voices would shout if they could, how much blood— less odious than this indifference—would redden these walls.)

In "La plaza" [The Square], a poem strikingly similar to others on the theme, José Angel Valente accentuates the feeling of oppression and loss, making of the square a totally empty space where every corner and stone speaks of a time gone and of loneliness. As in the other texts, attention is directed to the words pronounced in a rally: "Aquí alguien habló / tal vez a hombres unidos / en la misma esperanza." ("Here someone, perhaps, talked to men joined by the same hope," *P.C.,* 122). And because they all listened to the message of political hope, life must have been truly communal:

> Tal vez entonces
> tuvo en verdad la vida
> cauce común y fue la patria
> un nombre más extenso
> de la amistad o del amor.
>   Aquí
> latía un solo corazón unánime.

(Then perhaps life had truly a common current and the motherland was a wider name for friendship or love. Here a single, unanimous heart throbbed.)

But then, all of that was before, when people went to the square, when there was a reason for doing it. The postwar poet finds only emptiness in the square, abandoned by those who neither see hope nor have the freedom to be part of their world. If for Aleixandre the public square was a bright image of man's destiny, for Valente it represents the barren aspect of a country deprived of its rights. But the square, no matter how empty it looks, still exists and waits for the people who someday will fill it once more with "sueños, repartidas faenas, / palabras pronunciadas / con idética fe" ("dreams, shared chores, words pronounced with identical faith").

Chapter Nine
Conclusion

Toward the end of the 1960s the predominance of social poetry in Spain began to ebb. Among the most evident indications of the diminishing interest in social poetry is the evolution, or notable change, visible in Celaya's new books, be they poems or criticism. A well-accepted sign also is the anthology *Nueve novísimos poetas españoles* [Nine Very New Spanish Poets, 1970], prepared by José María Castellet, the same critic who a decade earlier had been partially responsible for popularizing the social poets and the theoretical basis of their works. The new twist in Spanish poetry in the 1970s is also documented in two special issues of the magazine *Cuadernos para el diálogo*. The first one, entitled "Treinta años de literatura en España" [Thirty Years of Literature in Spain], published in May 1969, considers that year as the end point of a literary period; the second special issue, "Literatura española a treinta años del siglo XXI" [Spanish Literature Thirty Years Before the Twenty-First Century], appeared in December 1970 and clearly established that year as the point of departure of a new literature.

Although these editorial manipulations cannot in themselves describe the evolution of poetry in contemporary Spain, they certainly dramatize the changes brought to all forms of literature by the new economic, political, and cultural conditions in a country then reaching the final stages in a long process of adaptation to postwar Europe. It also shows how Spanish literature continues to be an important factor in the political development of the country, as it has been for the last forty years.

Social poetry was born at a moment in Spain's history when the national conscience was being undermined by the very effective propaganda of a dictatorship that knew how to use the available means of mass communication for its own convenience. The first social poets believed themselves able to compete with their art against this generalized misinformation, becoming public figures, popular poets who had to transform and limit drastically their poetic diction in order to reach the public. This situation was, from the start, condemned to failure because of the new developments in the mass media and the consequent changes in taste among the public.

In a conversation concerning the future of poetry published in the second special issue of *Cuadernos para el diálogo,* Gabriel Celaya indicates the basis of the conflict confronting the social poet in our days:

I think there are two tendencies in present poetry which do not correspond to literary fashions, and that in each of these two tendencies it is possible to discern several literary schools. There is, certainly, that one we call basically the new *Mester de Juglaría,* and a new *Mester de Clerecía.* What is this new *Mester de Juglaría?* A poetry that has originated out of the need for access to the masses; the poets are youngsters who play the guitar and sing poems . . . and who, undoubtedly, reach a large public; they are the modern equivalent of the old *jongleur* made possible today by the new means of aural transmission.

Conversely, the old *Mester de Clerecía* has its modern equivalent in the contemporary experimental poetry, which can only be for the minority. For the social poet who wanted to reach a wide public, this distinction threatened again (thanks to the modern technology and economics) the loss of all hope for popularity. As Angel González comments on the same occasion: "I would like very much to know how to compose songs, but I am not able to do it. That possibility has arrived too late in my life, perhaps because I am already 'deformed' by the craft of the clergy."

The realization that poetry is not a popular form of artistic communication affects the style of the younger social poets who wrote for a reading public, and explains the silence of other poets who wrote social poetry as long as this was considered of public interest, but stopped when the public turned to the singers who conveyed the same message in an artistic medium with which the common people could relate more directly. The new *jongleurs* count among them those who sing social poetry, whether taken from well-known poets or written by themselves, as the natural complement of their folkloric melodies.

Only a few social poets continued writing into the 1970s, but their works have become highly complex and markedly literary. They do not abandon their political and social convictions, but they understand that their duty to society does not require from them what they cannot do as poets. Social poetry fought against poetic formalism and social injustice; by so doing, it introduced a new language and a new view of reality, thus leaving open ground to a development its authors probably never envisioned—the revival of oral poetry in popular and folkloric songs. Written poetry withdrew once more to its own aesthetically demanding domain; it took with it the enriched sense of commitment to social man.

Notes and References

Chapter One

1. See Juan Cano Ballesta, *La poesía española entre pureza y revolución (1930–1936)* (Madrid: Gredos, 1972); J. Lechner, *El compromiso en la poesía española del siglo XX.* Parte Primera (Leiden, 1968); John Butt, *Writers and Politics in Modern Spain* (London, 1978), and Natalia Calamai, *El compromiso en la poesía de la guerra civil española* (Barcelona: Editorial Laia, 1979).

2. Fanny Rubio, *Les revistas poéticas españolas (1939–1975)* (Madrid: Turner, 1976), pp. 28–35, 108–21.

3. See Charles D. Ley, *Spanish Poetry Since 1939* (Washington, D.C., 1962).

4. Manuel Durán, "Spanish Literature Since the War," in *On Contemporary Literature,* ed R. Kostelanetz (New York, 1969), pp. 193–202; Guillermo de Torre, "Contemporary Spanish Poetry," *Texas Quarterly* 4, no. 1 (1961):55–78. For a different view, see Ley, *Spanish Poetry,* pp. 37–49.

5. Leopoldo de Luis, "Otro acercamiento a *Sombra del Paraíso,"* *Sagitario* 1 (1971):9.

6. Vicente Aleixandre, *Obras completas* (Madrid, 1968), pp. 519–21.

7. The bibliography on Aleixandre is very extensive. The English-speaking reader will find helpful information in *Vicente Aleixandre: A Critical Appraisal,* ed. Santiago Daydí-Tolson (Ypsilanti, Mich.: Bilingual Press/Editorial Bilingüe, 1981). See also Kessel Schwartz, *Vicente Aleixandre,* in the Twayne World Authors Series.

8. Dámaso Alonso, *Ensayos sobre poesía española* (Madrid: Revista de Occidente, 1944), pp. 351–93.

9. Dámaso Alonso, *Poemas escogidos* (Madrid, 1969), pp. 193–94. Further references to this edition will be indicated in the text in parentheses with the abbreviation *P.E.*

10. Carlos Bousoño, "La poesía de Dámaso Alonso," *Papeles de Son Armadans* 11 (1958):256–300; and Andrew P. Debicki, *Dámaso Alonso* (New York: Twayne Publishers, 1970).

11. *Espadaña. Revista de Poesía y Crítica (1944–1951)* (León, 1979), facsimile edition of the forty-eight numbers of the review with preliminary texts by the founders and editors: Antonio G. de Lama, Victoriano Crémer, and Eugenio de Nora. Further references will be to this edition. See also

Victor G. de la Concha, *La poesía española de posguerra* (Madrid, 1973) pp. 304–420; Lechner, *El compromiso,* Parte Segunda (Leiden, 1975), pp. 31–57; and Fanny Rubio, *Las revistas poéticas españolas* (1939–1975), pp. 256–72.

12. Antonio G. de Lama, "Poesía: impopularidad," *Espadaña* 8:189.

13. Victoriano Crémer, "Poetas en crisis," *Espadaña* 46:969.

14. Antonio G. de Lama, "Si Garcilaso volviera," *Espadaña,* p. xxxv. This text was originally published in *Cisneros* 6 (1943):122–24.

15. Eugenio de Nora, "Poética," *Espadaña,* 7:143.

16. Victoriano Crémer, in *Cisneros* 6 (1943), cited by de la Concha, *La poesía española,* pp. 310–11.

17. Victoriano Crémer, "España limita al este . . . ." *Espadaña* 1:10.

18. Victoriano Crémer, "Poética," in Leopoldo de Luis, ed., *Poesía social. Antología (1939–1968)* (Madrid, 1969), p. 72.

19. De la Concha, *La poesía española,* pp. 414–20.

20. Victoriano Crémer, *Poesía total (1944–1966)* (Barcelona, 1967), pp. 46–47. Further references to this edition will be indicated in the text in parentheses with the abbreviation *P.T.*

21. De la Concha, *La poesía española,* pp. 397–403.

22. Ibid. pp. 368–69.

23. Eugenio G. de Nora, "Carta abierta a Victoriano Crémer," *Espadaña* 46:978–79.

24. De la Concha, *La poesía española,* p. 360.

25. De Nora, "Carta abierta," p. 979. Cited by de la Concha, *La poesía española,* p. 359.

26. Eugenio G. de Nora, *Poesía (1939–1964)* (León, 1975), pp. 315–17. Further references to this edition will be indicated in the text in parentheses with the abbreviation *P.*

27. All the citations from this book, whose author was Eugenio de Nora, are taken from Manuel Lamana, "España y sus nuevos poetas," *Cuaderenos Americanos* 101, no. 6 (1958): 229–46.

Chapter Two

1. The poem "Patria" is from de Nora's book *España pasión de vida* [Spain, Passion for Life] (Barcelona: Instituto de Estudios Hispánicos, 1954) and is included in *Poesía,* p. 280.

2. Ildefonso-Manuel Gil's poems are cited from Lechner, *El compromiso,* pp. 147–51.

3. José Hierro's poetic works include seven volumes: *Tierra sin nosotros* [Land Without Us, 1946], *Alegría* [Joy, 1947], *Con las piedras, con el viento* [With the Stones, with the Wind, 1950], *Quinta del 42* [Draft Call of 42, 1953], *Estatuas yacentes* [Recumbent Statues, 1954], *Cuanto sé de mí* [All I Know about Myself, 1958], and *Libro de las alucinaciones* [Book of Hallucinations, 1964]. All of these, plus some uncollected poems, form the

volume *Cuanto sé de mí* (Barcelona, 1974). The poem "Ellos" appears on pages 76 to 78 of this edition.

4. Miguel Labordeta (1921–1969) published four volumes of poems, collected later in *Obras completas* (Zaragoza, 1972). "Mi antigua juvenil despedida" is from his book *Epilírica* (1961), and appears in *O.C.*, pp. 252–53.

5. Miguel Laborteda, "Poesía revolucionaria," *Espadaña* 47:1008; de la Concha, *La poesía española*, p. 362.

6. Included among the "Poemas últimos (1938–1941)," published for the first time in José Hernández, *Obra escogida* (Madrid: Aguilar, 1952).

7. From *Nuevos cantos de vida y esperanza* (1952), in Crémer, *Poesía total*, pp. 140–41.

8. Angela Figuera Aymerich, "La cárcel" [Jail], from *El grito inútil* (1952), included also in Angela Figuera Aymerich, *Antología total* (Madrid: C.V.S. Ediciones, 1975), pp. 59–60.

Chapter Three

1. See Max Gallo, *Spain Under Franco* (New York: Dutton, 1974), pp. 201–68.

2. Aleixandre, *Obras completas*, pp. 1570–80.

3. Bousoño, in his *Teoría de la expresión poética* (Madrid: Gredos, 1952), supports theoretically the idea that all poetry is a form of communication.

4. Aleixandre, *Obras completas*, p. 1570.

Chapter Four

1. Prologue to Blas de Otero, *Ancia* (Madrid: Visor, 1971), p. 11; previously in Alonso, *Poetas españoles contemporáneos* (Madrid: Gredos, 1952).

2. Blas de Otero, *Expresión y reunión (1941–1969)* (Madrid: Alfaguara, 1969), p. 16.

3. Blas de Otero, *Hacia la inmensa mayoría* (Buenos Aires: Losada, 1962), 44. This volume collects four of Otero's books: *Angel fieramente humano, Redoble de conciencia, Pido la paz y la palabra,* and *En castellano.* Further references to this edition will be indicated in the text in parentheses with the abbreviation *H.I.M.*

4. For a detailed study of some of these characteristics, see Emilio Alarcos Llorach, *La poesía de Blas de Otero,* 2d ed. (Salamanca: Anaya, 1973), and Moraima Semprún Donahue, *Blas de Otero en su poesía* (Chapel Hill, 1977).

5. Fernando Lázaro Carreter, *Estudios de poética* (Madrid: Taurus, 1976), pp. 55–58.

6. Otero's commentaries in *Antología consultada de la joven poesía española* (Valencia: n.p., 1952), p. 179.

7. Blas de Otero, "Impreso prisionero," *Que trata de España* (Madrid: Visor, 1977), p. 32. Further references to this book will be indicated in the text in parentheses with the abbreviation *Q.T.E.*

Chapter Five

1. For a study of Celaya's life and work, see Sharon Keefe Ugalde, *Gabriel Celaya* (Boston, Twayne Publishers 1978).
2. Celaya's introduction to the new edition of *Lo demás es silencio* (Madrid: Turner, 1976), pp. 7–8.
3. Gabriel Celaya, "Veinte años de poesía (1927–1947)," in *Poesía y verdad* (Pontevedra: Ediciones Litoral, 1959), p. 54.
4. Gabriel Celaya, *Poesías completas* (Madrid: Aguilar, 1969), pp. 828–35. There is another edition, in eleven volumes of *Poesías completas* (Barcelona, 1977, 1978). Further references are to the 1969 edition and are indicated in parentheses with the abbreviation *P.C.*
5. Eugenio Matus, "El mundo poético de Juan de Leceta," *Cuadernos Hispanoamericanos* 314–15 (1976):455–94.
6. Gabriel Celaya, "Historia de mis libros," in *Itinerario poético* (Madrid: Ediciones Cátedra, 1975), p. 23.
7. Gabriel Celaya, *Lo demás es silencio* (Madrid: Turner, 1976), p. 7.
8. Written in Cuba in 1967–68, it was not published until it appeared as the fourth section of *Dirección prohibida* (Buenos Aires: Losada, 1973), pp. 113–30.
9. Ugalde, *Gabriel Celaya*, p. 83.
10. See the poem "La arcilla que palpo y beso," *P.C.*, pp. 602–4.
11. See, in particular, his book *Paz y concierto* (1953).

Chapter Six

1. Manuel Tuñón de Lara, *Antonio Machado, poeta del pueblo* (Barcelona: Editorial Terra Nova, 1967), pp. 309–28.
2. In 1952 Arturo del Hoyo prepared an edition of Miguel Hernández, *Obra escogida,* that includes the unpublished poems Hernández wrote in prison. Some of his poems were published in *Espadaña* and other literary periodicals. See Fanny Rubio, *Revistas poéticas españolas* (Madrid: Turner, 1976), passim.
3. Lechner, *El compromiso,* Segunda Parte pp. 66–85.
4. De Luis, *Poesía social,* p. 10.
5. Angela Figuera Aymerich, *Antología total* (Madrid, 1975), p. 24. Further references to this edition are indicated in the text in parentheses with the abbreviation *A.T.*
6. Manuel Gerena sings his politically inspired poems in the style of *cante jondo.* The texts of these compositions have been published in three volumes: *Antología de Manuel Gerena* (Madrid: Akal Editor, 1978), *Cantando*

a la libertad (Madrid, 3d ed.: Aral Editor, 1976), and *Cantes del pueblo para el pueblo* (Barcelona: Editorial Laia, 1977).

7. In his prologue to Gloria Fuertes, *Antología poética (1950–1969)* (Barcelona, 1975), Francisco Ynduraín insists upon the oral quality of her poetry, and even indicates on page 38 that "the reader will lose some essential aspect of these books if he has not been able to listen to them in the voice of the author herself."

8. Fuertes, *Antología poética,* p. 193. Further references to this edition are indicated in the text in parentheses with the abbreviation *A.P.*

9. There are several critical studies about this group, and each one gives it a different designation: Josep Batlló, *Antología de la nueva poesía española* (Madrid, 1968); Juan García Hortelano, *El grupo poético de los años cincuenta* (Madrid, 1978); Antonio Hernández, *Una promoción desheredada: La poética del cincuenta* (Bilbao, 1978); José Olivio Jiménez, "Poética y poesía de la joven generación española," *Hispania* 49 (1966): 195–205; José Marra-López, "Una nueva generación poética," *Insula* 221 (1965):5; Florencio Martínez Ruiz, *La nueva poesía española. Segunda generación de postguerra* (Madrid, 1971); Philip Silver, "New Spanish Poetry: The Rodríguez-Brines Generation," *Books Abroad* 42, no. 1 (1968):211–14; and Rubén Vela, *Ocho poetas españoles. Generación del Realismo Social* (Buenos Aires, 1965).

10. A second edition of this work, revised and enlarged, appeared later with the title of *Un cuarto de siglo de poesía española* (Barcelona, 1966).

11. Alfonso Sastre, "¿Qué es el social-realismo?" *Indice de Artes y Letras* 51 (1952):15–16.

12. Alfonso Sastre, *Anatomía del realismo* (Barcelona: Seix Barral, 1965), pp. 20–21.

13. Castellet, *Un cuarto,* p. 109.

14. José Marra-López, "La colección Colliure. Poesía de compromiso," *Insula* 183 (1962):4.

15. Lechner, *El compromiso,* Segunda Parte p. 85.

16. Castellet, *Un cuarto,* p. 109.

Chapter Seven

1. Aleixandre, *Obras completas,* p. 1532.

2. Carlos Barral, "Poesía no es comunicación," *Laye* 23 (1953):23–26.

3. Jaime Gil de Biedma, "Poesía y comunicación," *Cuadernos Hispanoamericanos* 67 (1955):96–101.

4. Ricardo Paseyro, "Poesía, poetas y antipoetas. Conocimiento y poesía," *Indice de Artes y Letras* 120 (1959):21.

5. *Obras completas,* pp. 1535–36.

6. See Chapter 6, note 9.

7. In *Poesía última* (Madrid: Taurus, 1963), pp. 155–61; reproduced, with certain changes, in José Angel Valente's collection of essays, *Las palabras de la tribu* (Madrid: Siglo Veintiuno, 1971), pp. 3–10.

8. J. A. Goytisolo, *Salmos al viento* (Barcelona, 4th ed., 1973), pp. 39–42.

9. M. Caballero Bonald, "Cuando estas palabras escribo," in *Vivir para contarlo* (Barcelona, 1969), p. 55. The poetic works of Caballero Bonald include *Las adivinaciones* (Madrid, 1952); *Memorias de poco tiempo* (Madrid, 1954); *Anteo* (Palma de Mallorca, 1956); *Las horas muertas* (Barcelona, 1959); *Pliegos de cordel* (Barcelona, 1963). All of these are collected in *Vivir para contarlo*, together with other compositions later added to *Descrédito del héroe* (Barcelona, 1977).

10. J. A. Valente, *Punto cero: Poesía 1953–1979* (Barcelona, 1980), p. 165. This volume collects all previously published books: *A modo de esperanza* (Madrid, 1955); *Poemas a Lázaro* (Madrid, 1960); *La memoria y los signos* (Madrid, 1966); *Presentación y memorial para un monumento* (Madrid, 1970); *El inocente* (México, 1970); *Treinta y siete fragmentus* (Barcelona, 1972); *Interior con figuras* (Barcelona, 1976); and *Material Memorial* (Barcelona, 1979).

11. See S. Daydí-Tolson, "Los efectos de la resonancia en la poesía de José Angel Valente," in *The Analysis of Hispanic Texts: Current Trends in Methodology*. Third and Fourth York College Colloquiums (New York: Bilingual Press/Editorial Bilingüe, 1979).

12. A. González, *Palabra sobre palabra* (Barcelona, 1972), p. 46. This volume collects all the books published previously by the poet: *Áspero mundo* (Madrid, 1956); *Sin esperanza, con convencimiento* (Barcelona, 1961); *Grado elemental* (Paris, 1962); *Tratado de urbanismo* (Barcelona, 1967); *Breves acotaciones para una biografía* (Las Palmas, 1969); *Procedimientos narrativos* (Santander, 1962); a later book is *Muestra, corregida y aumentada de algunos procedimientos narrativos y de las actitudes sentimentales que habitualmente comportan* (Madrid: Ediciones Turner, 1977).

13. J. M. Caballero Bonald, "Comentario en torno al realismo de la nueva poesía española," *Revista de la Universidad de los Andes* 3, no. 11–12 (1960):37–44; "Vigencia de la poesía de Blas de Otero," *Papeles de Son Armadans* 1, no. 1 (1956):114–18; and "Gabriel Celaya: Poesía (1934–1961)," *Insula* 190 (1962):5.

14. J. A. Valente, "Conocimiento y comunicación," in *Poesía última*, p. 159.

15. J. A. Valente, *Las palabras de la tribu*, pp. 11–15.

16. Carlos Barral, *Cuadernos para el diálogo*, XIV Extraordinario: "Treinta años de literatura: Narrativa y poesía española, 1939–1969" (1969):39–42.

17. J. A. Valente, "Segundo homenaje a Isidore Ducasse," in *Punto cero*, p. 294.

18. For a study of versification in Angel González's works see Emilio Alarcos Llorach, *Angel González, poeta* (Oviedo, 1969). In *Poesía social: Un caso español contemporáneo* (Valparaíso, 1969) I study the metric combinations common to Valente's style.

19. Jaime Gil de Biedma, *Las personas del verbo* (Barcelona, 1975), p. 27. This book collects all of Gil de Biedma's poems published previously in four volumes: *Según sentencia del tiempo* (Barcelona, 1953); *Compañeros de viaje* (Barcelona, 1959); *Moralidades* (México, 1966); and *Poemas póstumos* (Madrid, 1968).

Chapter Eight

1. For a personal account of the postwar years by one of the leading literary figures of the younger generation see C. Barral, *Años de penitencia. Memorias* (Madrid: Alianza Editorial, 1975), and *Los años sin excusa. Memorias II* (Barcelona: Barral Editores, 1978).

2. In response to a questionnaire in Hernández, *Una promoción desheredada: la poética del cincuenta*, p. 309.

3. Valente, *Punto cero*, pp. 31–34.

4. Caballero Bonald, *Vivir para contarlo*, pp. 226–27.

5. Gil de Biedma, *Las personas del verbo*, pp. 19–20.

6. Goytisolo, *Salmos al viento*, pp. 105–6.

7. González, "El invierno" [Winter], *Palabra sobre palabra*, p. 90.

8. Carlos Sahagún's works include only three books of poems: *Profecías del agua* (Madrid, 1957); *Como si hubiera muerto un niño* (Barcelona, 1961); and *Estar contigo* (León, 1973). All of these are collected, together with a few unpublished compositions, in *Memorial de la noche* (Barcelona, 1976).

9. Sahagún, "Visión de Almería," *Memorial de la noche*, p. 108.

10. Sahagún, untitled poem, *Memorial de la noche*, p. 15.

11. González, "El invierno," *Palabra sobre palabra*, p. 90.

12. Sahagún, "Palabras junto a un lago," *Memorial de la noche*, p. 71.

13. Aleixandre, *Obras completas*, pp. 711–13.

14. González, "Plaza con torreones y palacios," *Palabra sobre palabra*, pp. 217–18.

Selected Bibliography

PRIMARY SOURCES

1. In English

Alonso, Dámaso. *Hijos de la ira—Children of Wrath*. Translated by Elias L. Rivers. Baltimore: The Johns Hopkins Press, 1970.

Baland, Timothy, and St. Martin, Hardie, eds. *Miguel Hernández and Blas de Otero: Selected Poems*. Boston: Beacon Press, 1972. Bilingual edition.

Hyde, Lewis, ed. *A Longing for the Light. Selected Poems of Vicente Aleixandre*. New York: Harper & Row, 1979.

St. Martin, Hardie, ed. *Roots and Wings. Poetry from Spain 1900–1975*. New York: Harper & Row, 1976. Bilingual anthology. A few social poets are represented: Gabriel Celaya, Blas de Otero, Gloria Fuertes, José Hierro, Angel González, José Angel Valente, Jaime Gil de Biedma, and Carlos Sahagún.

Walsh, Donald D., trans. *Angel González: "Harsh World" and Other Poems*. Princeton: Princeton University Press, 1976.

2. In Spanish
a. Anthologies

Antología Consultada de la Joven Poesía Española. Valencia: n.p., 1952.

Batlló, José, ed. *Antología de la nueva poesía española*. Madrid: El Bardo, 1968. Introductory study, and poet's answers to a questionnaire about poetry.

Cano, José Luis, ed. *El tema de España en la poesía española contemporánea*. Madrid: Revista de Occidente, 1964. Anthology and introductory study about the subject of Spain in Spanish poetry from the nineteenth century to the 1960s.

Castellet, José María, ed. *Un cuarto de siglo de poesía española*. Barcelona: Seix Barral, 4th ed., 1966. Anthology preceded by a long, polemical study about twentieth-century Spanish poetry in which the author underlines the new developments of social realism in poetry as a style superseding symbolism.

De Luis, Leopoldo, ed. *Poesía Social. Antología (1939–1968)*. Madrid: Alfaguara, 2d ed., 1969. Brief and not-too-informative introduction. The poets comment about social poetry.

García Hortelano, Juan, ed. *El grupo poético de los años 50.* Madrid: Taurus, 1978. Very informative introductory study about the poets of the 1950s. Ample anthology.

Hernández, Antonio, ed. *Una promoción desheredada: La poética del cincuenta.* Bilbao: Zero, 1978. Confusing introductory study to a representative anthology. Poets' answers to a questionnaire.

Martínez Ruiz, Florencio, ed. *La nueva poesía española. Segunda generación de postguerra, 1955–1970. Antología crítica.* Madrid: Biblioteca Nueva, 1971. Very helpful critical introduction.

Ribes, Francisco, ed. *Poesía última.* Madrid: Taurus, 1963. Anthology of five poets—Eladio Cabañero, Angel González, Claudio Rodríguez, Carlos Sahagún, and José Angel Valente—and their commentaries about poetry. Brief introductory study.

Vela, Rubén, ed. *Ocho poetas españoles. Generación del Realismo Social.* Buenos Aires: Dead Weight, 1965. Includes poems and comments about poetry by Carlos Barral, José Manual Caballero Bonald, Gabino-Alejandro Carriedo, Angel Crespo, Jaime Gil de Biedma, Angel González, José Agustín Goytisolo, and José Angel Valente.

b. Individual Authors

Aleixandre, Vicente. *Obras completas.* Madrid: Aguilar, 1978.

Alonso, Dámaso. *Poemas escogidos.* Madrid: Gredos, 1969.

Caballero Bonald, José Manuel. *Vivir para contarlo.* Barcelona: Barral, 1969.

————. *Descrédito del héroe.* Barcelona: El Bardo, 1977.

Celaya, Gabriel. *Poesías completas.* Barcelona: Editorial Laia, 1977–1978. Eleven volumes.

Crémer, Victoriano. *Poesía total. 1944–1966.* Barcelona: Plaza y Janés, 1967.

De Nora, Eugenio (García). *Poesía (1939–1964).* León: Institución "Fray Bernardino de Sahagún," 1975.

Figuera Aymerich, Angela. *Antología total (1948–1969).* Madrid: C.V.S. Ediciones, 1975.

Fuertes, Gloria. *Antología poética (1950–1969).* Barcelona: Plaza y Janés, 3d ed., 1975.

Gil de Biedma, Jaime. *Las personas del verbo.* Barcelona: Barral, 1975.

González, Angel. *Palabra sobre palabra.* Barcelona: Barral, 1972.

————. *Muestra, corregida y aumentada, de algunos procedimientos narrativos y de las actitudes sentimentales que habitualmente comportan.* Madrid: Turner, 1977.

Goytisolo, José Agustín. *El retorno.* Madrid: Adonais, 1955.

————. *Salmos al viento.* Barcelona: Ocnos, 1973.

————. *Claridad.* Valencia: Diputación Provincial, 1961.

————. *Años decisivos.* Barcelona: Colliure, 1961.

————. *Algo sucede.* Madrid: El Bardo, 1968.

————. *Bajo tolerancia.* Barcelona: Ocnos, 1973.

————. *Taller de arquitectura.* Barcelona: Editorial Lumen, 1977.

————. *Del tiempo y del olvido.* Barcelona: Editorial Lumen, 1977.

Hierro, José. *Cuanto sé de mí.* Barcelona: Seix Barral, 1974.

Labordeta, Miguel. *Obras completas.* Zaragoza: Ediciones Javalambre, 1972.

Otero, Blas de. *Expresión y reunión.* Madrid: Alfaguara, 1969.

————. *Expresion y reunión.* Madrid: Alianza Editorial, 1981.

————. *Verso y prosa.* Madrid: Ediciones Cátedra, 1976.

Sahagún, Carlos. *Memorial de la noche.* Barcelona: El Bardo, 1976.

Valente, José Angel. *Punto cero.* Barcelona: Seix Barral, 1980.

————. *El fin de la edad de plata.* Barcelona: Seix Barral, 1973.

SECONDARY SOURCES

1. In English

Batlló, José. "An Introduction to 'New Spanish Poetry.' " *Mundus Artium* 2, no. 2 (1969):66–71. General information about the poets who began publishing around 1950. An introduction to the developments of Spanish poetry in the 1950s and 1960s.

Bosch, Rafael. "The New Nonconformist Spanish Poetry." *Odyssey Review* 2, no. 2 (1962):222–34. The works of the first social poets interpreted as a reaction to the conformist attitude of many postwar Spanish poets.

Bowra, C. M. *Poetry and Politics: 1900–1960.* Cambridge: At the University Press, 1966. Survey of European political poetry, including Spanish poets.

Butt, John. *Writers and Politics in Modern Spain.* London: Hodder and Stoughton, 1978. Good introduction to social poetry. It deals with twentieth-century developments of committed literature in Spain.

Cobb, Carl W. *Contemporary Spanish Poetry (1898–1963).* Boston: Twayne Publishers, 1976. General survey of twentieth-century Spanish poetry with little attention to postwar poets.

Cohen, J. M. "Since the Civil War: New Currents in Spanish Poetry." *Encounter* 65 (1959):44–53. A very general introduction to the different poetic manifestations in postwar Spain.

Correa, Gustavo. "Temporality and Commitment in Spanish Poetry After 1936." *Ventures: Magazine of the Yale Graduate School* 10, no. 1 (1970):33–36. Brief note relating historical circumstances to the commitment of Spanish poets during the decades following the civil war.

Durán, Manuel. "Spanish Literature Since the War." In *On Contemporary Literature.* Edited by R. Kostelanetz. New York: Avon Books, 2d printing, 1969, pp. 193–203. Brief general introduction to postwar Spanish letters, followed by a very selective reading list. Of interest to people not acquainted with Spanish literature.

Ilie, Paul. "The Disguises of Protest: Contemporary Spanish Poetry." *Michigan Quarterly Review* 10, no. 1 (1971):38–48. Important article because it poses several critical problems in relation to the true value of social poetry in Franco's Spain.

Ley, Charles David. *Spanish Poetry Since 1939.* Washington, D.C.: The Catholic University of America Press, 1962. Informative discussion of postwar poetic developments in Spain. Poems analyzed. Bibliographies.

Mandlove, Nancy B. "Feminine Voice of the Post War." In *Conference on Hispanic Languages and Literatures.* Edited by J. C. Mendizábal. Indiana: Indiana University of Pennsylvania, 1976, pp. 176–83. Too praising commentary about the poets' style and thematics. Stresses feminism and social commitment.

Silver, Philip W. "New Spanish Poetry: The Rodríguez-Brines Generation." *Books Abroad* 42, no. 2 (1968):211–14. The young Spanish poets who published their first works in the 1950s represent a comeback to the best poetry of the years preceding the civil war.

St. Martin, Hardie. "Poetry in Spain Since the Civil War." *Mosaic: A Journal for the Comparative Study of Literature and Ideas* 2, no. 4 (1968):41–52. General outline of the different poetic trends in postwar Spain.

Torre, Guillermo de. "Contemporary Spanish Poetry." *Texas Quarterly* 4, no. 1 (1961):55–78. General review of Spanish poetry in the twentieth century, including postwar poets.

Ugalde, Sharon Keefe. *Gabriel Celaya.* Boston: Twayne Publishers, 1978. Detailed study of Celaya's life and works. It has a chapter on Celaya's social poetry. Selected bibliography.

Yglesias, José. *The Franco Years.* New York: Bobbs-Merrill Co. 1977. Conversations with Spaniards from different professions. Good human document with little historical and critical commentary. A must for those interested in everyday life in Franco Spain. There is one chapter devoted to Gabriel Celaya.

2. In Spanish

Alarcos Llorach, Emilio. *Angel González, poeta.* Oviedo: Universidad de Oviedo, 1969. Complete study of the poet's work, with analysis of techniques and inspiring ideas. Good introduction to the detailed study of the poets of the 1950s.

————. *La poesía de Blas de Otero.* Salamanca: Ediciones Anaya, 2d ed., 1973. Concise and complete analysis of Blas de Otero's style and its motivations.

Aub, Max. *Una nueva poesía española, 1950–1955.* México: Imprenta Universitaria, 1957. A series of lectures intended to inform the general public about the new developments in Spanish poetry in the early 1950s. Informative and detailed, it offers many examples of poetry by authors not otherwise well known.

Blanco Aguinaga, Carlos; Rodríguez Puértolas, Julio; and Zavala, Iris M. *Historia social de la literatura española (en lengua castellana).* Madrid: Editorial Castalia, 1979. Three volumes dedicated to a reappraisal of Spanish literature from a sociological point of view. Of great help in understanding postwar social poetry, although the treatment of individual writers is uneven and far from novel.

Castellet, José María. *Literatura, ideología y política.* Barcelona: Editorial Anagrama, 1976. Series of articles about committed literature at the present time by a leading theorist of Social Realism in Spain.

Ciplijauskaité, Biruté. *El poeta y la poesía.* Madrid: Insula, 1966. A complete survey of ideas about poetry among contemporary Spanish poets. A chapter devoted to the postwar period offers a careful study of the theoretical basis of social poetry.

Daydí-Tolson, Santiago. *Poesía social: Un caso español contemporáneo.* Valparaíso: Universidad Católica de Valparaíso, 1969. Brief monograph about the poetics of social poetry as represented by one of José Angel Valente's poems.

————. "La poética de lo social: *Sobre el lugar del canto* de José Angel Valente." *Journal of Spanish Studies Twentieth Century* 6, no. 1 (1978):3–11. The social value of poetry depends on its ability to renew language and thus unveil the truth.

De la Concha, Víctor G. *La poesía española de posguerra. Teoría de sus movimientos.* Madrid: Editorial Prensa Española, 1973. An exhaustive study of Spanish poetry during the ten years following the war, and its immediate antecedents. Bibliography.

Donahue, Moraima de Semprún. *Blas de Otero en su poesía.* Chapel Hill: University of North Carolina Press, 1977. Very technical study of Otero's works; it is divided in sections about themes, metaphors, symbols, images, and style in general. Bibliography.

Gimferrer, Pedro. "La poesía de Jaime Gil de Biedma." *Cuadernos Hispanoamericanos* 202 (1966):240–45. Gil de Biedma's works are ethical in essence and represent the maturity of a new style, that of the younger generation of the 1950s.

González Muela, Joaquín. *La nueva poesía española.* Madrid: Ediciones Alcalá, 1973. Series of articles on individual poets—Gloria Fuertes,

Angel González, José Angel Valente, Claudio Rodríguez, Jaime Gil de Biedma, Manuel Vázquez Montalbán, and Pere Gimferrer. Review of several anthologies of contemporary Spanish poetry. General considerations about the new poets.

Grande, Félix. *Apuntes sobre poesía española de posguerra.* Madrid: Taurus, 1970. Critical review of postwar poetry in Spain. Very informative.

Jiménez, José Olivio. *Diez años de poesía española: 1960–1970.* Insula: Madrid, 1972. Series of critical essays on individual writers and particular books published during the period under study. General introduction stressing the overcoming of social poetry and the theory of poetry as communication among Spanish poets.

Lechner, J. *El compromiso en la poesía española del siglo XX. Parte Segunda: De 1934 a 1974.* Leiden: Universitaire Pers Leiden, 1975. The most complete study of social poetry; it offers valuable information, bibliographies, and texts related to political writing in the forty years of Franco's regime.

Marra-López, José. "Una nueva generación poética." *Insula* 221 (1965):5. The younger poets of the 1950s continue the humanization of poetry as seen in Blas de Otero and follow two currents—one of social poetry, the other espousing solidarity with all men. General characterization of the new poets.

Rodríguez Padrón, Jorge. "Años decisivos para la poesía de José Agustín Goytisolo." *Cuadernos Hispanoamericanos* 232 (1969):236–51. Goytisolo, like the rest of the poets of the generation of 1950, writes poetry based upon the historical experience of the war. A review of the poet's work helps to understand his social commitment and his particular style.

Siebenmann, Gustav. *Los estilos poéticos en España desde 1900.* Madrid: Gredos, 1973. Social poetry is seen as part of a wider view of contemporary Spanish poetry. This book gives a complete and coherent exposition of the different periods and styles in the Spanish poetry of the twentieth century.

Index